Cleaner LIVING

How to Build Decluttering
& Home Organization Habits
That Last

EMILY HART

Legal Notice

This book aims to provide general information, personal insights, and motivational guidance on decluttering, home organization, and habit formation. While every effort has been made to ensure the accuracy and relevance of the content, Emily Hart and the publisher make no representations or warranties—express or implied—regarding the completeness, reliability, effectiveness, or suitability of the information provided.

Readers are encouraged to exercise their best judgment and consult appropriate professionals when making significant changes to their living space, lifestyle, or mental health routines. The author and publisher are not responsible for any injuries, losses, damages, or adverse outcomes resulting from the use or misuse of the material presented in this book.

All product names, logos, brands, and trademarks mentioned herein are the property of their respective owners. References to these products or services are included for informational purposes only and do not imply any affiliation, sponsorship, or endorsement.

Disclaimer

The strategies, tips, and ideas in this book derive from the author's personal experiences, research, and opinions. While these insights aim to assist readers in developing lasting decluttering and organization habits, individual results may vary, and no specific outcomes are guaranteed.

The methods outlined in this book may not suit everyone. Readers are encouraged to assess their situations and seek advice from qualified professionals—such as therapists, organizers, or healthcare providers—when necessary.

By reading and using this book, you acknowledge and agree that neither the author nor the publisher is liable for any consequences, directly or indirectly, arising from the application of the information contained herein. Your actions and decisions are your own responsibility.

Digital Detox Workbook

Your 7-Day Guide to Reducing Digital Clutter

Please scan this code for a free copy of our **Digital Detox Workbook**

This workbook will guide you through a 7-day digital detox journey, helping you reduce digital clutter, regain focus, and build healthier tech habits for a calmer, more intentional digital life. Get started today.

Contents

Introduction   1

Section 1

LAYING THE GROUNDWORK

Chapter 1
Understanding Clutter   7

Chapter 2
The Psychology of Habits   15

Chapter 3
Creating Your Vision for a Cleaner Life   23

Section 2

DECLUTTERING FOUNDATIONS

Chapter 4
The 5 Decluttering Principles   29

Chapter 5
The Declutter Kickstart   37

Chapter 6
Letting Go Without Guilt   45

Section 3

BUILDING DAILY ORGANIZATION HABITS

Chapter 7
Daily Clean Habits for Every Room   51

Chapter 8
Systems That Simplify   59

Chapter 9

Your Weekly Reset Ritual   67

Section 4

LIFESTYLE INTEGRATION

Chapter 10

Mindful Consumption   77

Chapter 11

Family & Roommate Buy-In   83

Chapter 12

When Life Gets Messy   89

Section 5

STAYING MOTIVATED FOR THE LONG HAUL

Chapter 13

Tracking Your Progress   97

Chapter 14

Inspiration & Maintenance   105

Conclusion

A Clean Home Is A Clear Mind   113

INTRODUCTION

Every time it began, there was only one sock on the floor by the bed without a pair. Not a huge deal. Then came the mystery container at the back of the refrigerator, half-used lotions, expired spices, receipts in the kitchen drawer, and piles of unsorted mail. It always seemed more like a gradual accumulation than a deliberate choice. One day, the house began to seem more like a burden than a haven.

You've probably experienced something similar: being in your own house and feeling overpowered by the mental and physical clutter. Perhaps your efforts to straighten up have simply made you feel more irritated. Maybe you've followed influencers with immaculate pantries and color-coded closets or watched organizing shows, and rather than feeling motivated, you felt discouraged. That guilt? You're not by yourself.

Our environment has a significant influence on our thoughts, emotions, and behavior. It goes beyond aesthetics and environments that are fit for Pinterest. It has to do with vitality, clarity, and a feeling of mastery. We think more clearly when our surroundings help us rather than deplete us. We get better sleep. We accomplish more. We are lighter.

It has scientific foundations as well. According to studies, clutter raises our bodies' levels of the stress hormone cortisol. It diverts our attention and impairs our capacity for concentration. An untidy mind frequently results from a cluttered environment. It's more difficult to unwind. More challenging to begin the day. Even when everything else in your life is going well, it can be challenging to feel like you've got it together. Additionally, when we are continuously exposed to minor stresses from our physical surroundings, they gradually accumulate. A thousand stacks of paper will kill you.

Then, there is the unstated expense of time. How much time do we spend rummaging through overflowing drawers, untangling cords, or looking for misplaced keys? Since things were never really orderly in the first place, how many hours have we spent cleaning rather than unwinding? Disorganization has an emotional cost that we hardly ever consider—an imperceptible toll on our vitality and tranquility.

The fact that this isn't a personal failure, however, is something that isn't often acknowledged. It's not your lack of discipline or laziness that's causing chaos in your home.

It's not because you didn't purchase the appropriate containers or adhere to the proper cleaning protocol. Frequently, it's because we were never instructed on how to develop behaviors related to our space genuinely. We are trained to clean up, but we are not given maintenance instructions. While we receive advice, we are not taught a mindset.

And that is the purpose of this book.

It isn't just another booklet on "how to clean your house in 15 minutes a day." This isn't about pretending your life is a carefully manicured Instagram feed or cleaning until you pass out. It's about a change—a method of viewing your house as a partner in your everyday existence rather than as an issue that has to be resolved. We alter our appearance in the world when we reinterpret our interaction with our surroundings. Simple, doable tactics based on a fresh perspective are the focus of this book: less pressure more progress.

You are aware of how powerful your surroundings maybe if you have ever entered a room and felt uneasy right away. And you understand the magic that exists in even minor adjustments if you've ever cleaned a corner and felt a little more hopeful all of a sudden. The idea that having a cleaner, more tranquil life involves far more than just possessions is what we're focusing on here. It has to do with self-respect. It has to do with purpose. It's about assuming responsibility for something that affects every aspect of our everyday life.

Those who are fed up with false promises and fast remedies should read this book. It's for people who have tried major weekend purges, chore charts, and minimalist challenges only to find themselves back in the same mess weeks later. Full-time parents, working professionals, creative types, caregivers, and everyone else who simply wants to feel a little more at ease in their own home are all eligible.

It is specifically designed for novices. Those who believe they were not present at the lesson where everyone learned how to maintain order. Those who question why others seem to have it so easy. When the doorbell rings, they are the ones who feel ashamed. This is a handbook for those who want better, not for those who strive for perfection.

This journey may begin with a crowded closet, a mountain of laundry, or a schedule full of obligations. This may seem like just another thing to add to your already full plate. We'll start small because of this. One habit at a time, one drawer, one shelf. You won't have to spend hours color-coding your life or emptying your entire wardrobe onto the bed. Our goal is to create real-world systems that support your real life, not the one you see on TV, and that develop with you.

You'll discover a mix of deeper mindset work and valuable tips in this book. You'll learn about the reasons behind clutter, including the stories we tell ourselves, the emotional bonds we make, and the ways that perfectionism can hold us back. Additionally, there are reflection prompts and check-ins to help you identify what is most important to you—not to make you feel bad. Having a clean place isn't the only objective; it's to have a functional place.

Creating a life where your house works for you rather than against you is more about design than it is about discipline. There will also be difficulties, as with any new habit. It will feel easy on some days, and it feels like you're starting again on others. But with each tiny step, you'll be creating something more resilient than immaculate counters: steadiness, self-assurance, and composure.

The following chapters are structured to help you navigate that procedure. Understanding your current surroundings and identifying what functions well and what doesn't will be your first step. The mental side of clutter will be discussed next, including the anxiety, guilt, and "what-ifs" that make things challenging to let go. We'll then go over how to make the most functional spaces in your house—kitchens, closets, bathrooms, and paper piles—more manageable. You'll discover how to create routines that are adaptable yet dependable, how to enlist the help of family members, and how to keep up your progress without being burned out.

We're not aiming for magazine-worthy, which is what makes our journey unique. Our goal is to make it livable. For tranquility. For feasible. For homes that are more than merely aesthetically pleasing.

Here, too, there is room for happiness. It is for honoring the sensation of entering a space and becoming immediately more rooted for getting just what you need by opening a drawer. Because your home seems in harmony with your life, you will be able to breathe better at the end of the day. These few moments of relaxation are essentials, not extravagance. They support everything else you do.

This is your opportunity to make your house work for you if you've ever felt that it wasn't. A place that lifts you up, not one that brings you down, is what you deserve. Routines that feel like punishment are not what you deserve; you deserve routines that heal you. Most importantly, you deserve the clarity that comes from understanding your needs, where things are, and that you're not stuck.

This is an invitation to empty the mind and clear the space. Let's approach it with love, gentleness, and purpose. Let's establish enduring habits that make sense for your lifestyle and identity, not because they are rigid.

Being someone else isn't the point here. One tiny change at a time, it's about coming home to yourself.

Greetings from your new beginning.

Section 1

LAYING THE GROUNDWORK

UNDERSTANDING CLUTTER

It begins quietly. A few too many coffee mugs crammed into the cupboard, a jacket slung over the back of a chair, and a donation box in the corner. We all move quickly in life. A hectic week becomes two. By the end of the month, the jacket had taken up residence, and the donation box would remain. Not because we're irresponsible, but instead because we've adjusted, we eventually lose sight of the gradual accumulation of junk. After passing the stacks and navigating the jumble, we finally come to terms with the visual cacophony. But there's more going on beneath that placid exterior.

It's never just objects that cause clutter. It's a narrative, a contemplation, a feeling. It reveals information about our past and our feelings for the future. It shows how we define comfort, how we make decisions, and how we respond to stress. This chapter examines the causes, manifestations, and distinctions between clutter and basic disarray. By comprehending clutter, we empower ourselves to control it—not just once, but permanently.

Emotional and Psychological Roots of Clutter

There is a trail of emotions behind every crowded drawer and overstuffed closet. These feelings are frequently the real obstacles to letting go. We don't want piles of unread magazines or 10 pairs of pants. The reason is because we have an emotional attachment to the things they stand for. Perhaps it's a sense of duty associated with a gift or shame over money spent. Maybe it's sentimentality, a fear of regret, or the conviction that we could need that particular item someday after years of ignoring it.

Clutter frequently conveys a sense of poverty. Emotional scarcity is as much as material scarcity. It can seem like a hedge against an uncertain future to hold onto things. The larger concern, "What if I'm not prepared for what's ahead?" is subdued by asking, "What if I need this again?" This way of thinking makes sense, particularly to people who have experienced hardship. However, it results in physical weight that is detrimental to our current selves.

Additionally, there is the delusion of potential. For the pastime, we never really took up. We kept crafts supplies. We keep exercise equipment for the future selves we aspire to. Not only do these objects occupy space, but they also contain dreams. It can feel like giving up when you let them go. More often than not, though, it's the first step in redefining what our current priorities are.

Emotional exhaustion and stress are also important factors. Our energy shifts inward at difficult times, such as sorrow, burnout, or transition. The last things on the list are purging, sorting, and tidying. Clutter turns into a tangible manifestation of the things we haven't had time to absorb. It can be simpler to overlook a disorganized shelf than to confront the feelings it contains.

Additionally, perfectionism is a silent clutter-keeper. Our dread of making a mistake can prevent us from taking any action at all. We never begin if we think a space must be perfectly ordered before we begin. Then, clutter turns into a holding pattern, a means of delaying choices until the ideal moment, which is rarely present.

Another important motivator is fear. Fear of forgetting, fear of wasting, fear of letting go, or worry of running out of things later. These anxieties have deep psychological roots and are frequently connected to family dynamics or prior experiences. Our inner narrative may associate decluttering with carelessness if we were raised in homes with little means or where nothing was wasted. We start accumulating "just in case," thinking we're being wise, but in reality, we're burdening our future selves excessively.

Clutter can occasionally be about identity. We hold on to things that remind us of who we were or who we hoped we would be. Books we never read but once intended to, clothes that no longer fit, and tools for long-forgotten hobbies. These objects take on symbolic meaning, binding us to a past self we find difficult to let go of completely. Even if that person no longer represents our reality, parting ways with them can feel like cutting off ties to who we were.

The burden is increased when clutter is connected to grief. Loved ones' possessions hold a presence in addition to memories. It can feel like deleting someone from your life when you let go of these things. This type of clutter must, therefore, be handled carefully, patiently, and compassionately. Forgetting is not the same as decluttering. It entails deciding which symbols and memories actually make today better.

The Different Types of Clutter

The phenomenon of clutter is not universal. Depending on where it resides and how it affects us, it takes on several personas. While some types are hidden in plain sight, others are readily apparent. We must comprehend the many categories and how they impact our well-being if we are to declutter effectively.

The most obvious type of clutter is physical. It's the overflowing drawers in the kitchen, the pile of books on the table, and the extra shoes in the foyer. It might be concentrated in forgotten areas or dispersed across every room. Physical clutter adds visual noise and adds weight to our dwellings. It slows down our daily activities, makes us more stressed, and makes it harder for us to unwind. Our minds detect the persistent presence of "too much," even if we're accustomed to it.

However, clutter extends beyond the boundaries of our shelves. The mind and heart are home to emotional clutter. It's the worry, remorse, and guilt we feel about our belongings. It's the burden of incomplete tasks, unfulfilled goals, and the expectation that we should be someone else. Physical objects can cause emotional clutter, but it can also exist on its own. It's the anxiety we harbor, the mental to-do lists we never finish, and the incessant criticism of ourselves.

Another more recent type of clutter that is equally draining is digital clutter. It manifests as cluttered desktop screens, unorganized photo collections, incessant phone notifications, and crowded inboxes. Our gadgets, which are meant to make our lives easier, may easily turn into stressors. Digital clutter keeps us distracted all the time, causes decision fatigue, and hinders focus. We often underestimate its influence because it's less visible. However, research indicates that the consequences of physical chaos can be mirrored by digital overload.

Calendar clutter, or the overscheduling of time and the lack of breathing room between commitments, is another expanding area. The same mental strain that physical disorders cause is created when every moment is planned, and our to-do list extends into tomorrow. There is little time for relaxation, introspection, or spontaneity when one's agenda is full. We lose presence when we are surrounded by this kind of clutter, which makes it more difficult to feel rooted in our own lives.

Relational clutter is equally real but more difficult to identify. It may manifest as one-sided friendships, unhealthy relationships, or incessant social media comparison. Just like a messy environment, emotional energy expended on squandering relationships takes up space. It prevents us from delving deeply into the important things. We frequently find that we need to emotionally clear out individuals and expectations that no longer serve us as we start to tidy our spaces.

Clutter of all kinds interacts with one another. Emotional overload is exacerbated by physical clutter. Digital chaos is fueled by procrastination, which is a result of emotional congestion. Additionally, our mental exhaustion is exacerbated by digital disarray. It turns into a vicious cycle that gradually depletes us until we take back control.

An important first step is to identify the kind of clutter we are dealing with. It gives us a clearer way to address the issue. We can remark, "I need to deal with my emotional attachment to this item," or "This digital space is making me feel scattered," as an alternative to feeling vaguely overwhelmed. That language moves us from helpless to intentional.

Clutter Versus Disorganization: Knowing the Difference

A common misperception is that disarray and clutter are synonymous. They're not. The first is about accumulation. The other concerns positioning. Knowing the difference enables us to choose the appropriate remedy for the appropriate problem.

Having too many items in one area, no matter how neatly they are arranged, is referred to as clutter. Even with bins, shelves, and containers labeled, there is simply too much to handle, and you may still feel overwhelmed. When we add more things to our lives than we use, need, or love, clutter results. The issue is one of volume.

Conversely, disorganization refers to a lack of structure. Despite their potential utility and significance, our possessions lack a home. They wind up strewn on counters, thrown into drawers, or lost as a result. Disorganization is more about where and how we store our possessions than it is about what we own. The issue is with the system.

Suppose you have strange screws, rubber bands, batteries, pens, and receipts in a kitchen drawer. That combines disarray and clutter. However, if you have fifteen different kinds of pens in a perfectly arranged drawer, many of which you never use, that is cluttered with structure. On the other hand, disarray without clutter is what happens if you only have one pen but lose it frequently.

This distinction is significant because we employ various methods to deal with them. The clutter has to be edited. It challenges us to assess what genuinely enriches our lives and let go of what doesn't. Systems are necessary for disarray. It invites us to give our possessions homes so we can easily locate and store them.

It's OK for some areas to suffer from both. The important thing is that we learn to distinguish between the two. We are better able to respond when we correctly identify the issue. We

make no effort to coordinate what ought to be donated. When all we actually need is a better system, we don't throw objects in exasperation.

Clutter and disarray reinforce one another when they coexist. Having too many things makes it difficult to maintain organization, and being disorganized makes the mess seem much more daunting. The end effect is a mind that reflects the chaotic feeling of the surroundings. Awareness is the first step in ending this pattern. It begins with a clear, shame-free view of our space.

Confusion and avoidance are breeding grounds for clutter. However, once we expose it—with interest rather than condemnation—we start to see the trends that made it possible for it to develop. We grow more self-aware, more deliberate in our decisions, and more assured of our capacity for transformation. Color-coded bins and containers don't provide clarity. It results from comprehension. And the most effective tool you'll use going ahead is that understanding.

Disorganization and clutter are commonplace. These are inherent aspects of being human. However, their definitions of our houses and lifestyles don't have to be. Knowing what we're really up against gives us the confidence to make deliberate, doable changes.

In this chapter, we have examined the various ways clutter appears in our lives and unearthed its deeper emotional causes. Additionally, we now know how to differentiate it from plain disarray, which can change the way we think about our environment. Building on this awareness and transforming understanding into action are the next steps. As we proceed, keep in mind that comprehending what has been preventing us from moving forward is just as important as cleaning up.

A clean room is a tool, not the ultimate objective. One that encourages presence, purpose, and tranquility in our day-to-day existence. One thoughtful decision at a time. Let's keep laying the groundwork that will enable this tool to serve your needs.

Bonus Materials

Understanding the nature of clutter is the foundation of cleaner living. It's not just about what's sitting on the kitchen counter—it's about what's weighing on your heart, distracting your mind, and draining your energy. These bonus materials will help you observe, reflect, and gently begin the process of letting go.

Clutter Reflection Checklist

Before decluttering, it helps to get curious. This checklist is your guide to understanding not just *what* you own but *why* you've kept it.

Clutter Reflection Checklist:

☐ I know what's in this drawer or shelf without opening it.

☐ I use or interact with this item regularly.

☐ This item supports my current lifestyle—not a past version of myself.

☐ I feel peace—not stress—when I see this item.

☐ I'm not holding onto this out of guilt, obligation, or fear.

☐ I know where this item belongs in my home.

☐ This item has a purpose I can clearly define.

☐ If I lost this item tomorrow, I wouldn't feel overwhelmed.

Use this checklist with one small area—like your bedside table, your purse, or a single drawer. Answer honestly, and observe what emotions come up. This isn't about tossing everything. It's about learning what matters most.

Weekly Clutter Awareness Habit Tracker

Understanding clutter begins with noticing it—not judging it. This simple habit tracker helps you tune into where and why clutter builds up during your week.

How to Use: At the end of each day, jot down one area where clutter is gathered. Use this space to reflect on what triggered it—a rushed morning? A stressful day? Lack of storage?

Day	Clutter Hotspot	Why It Happened	How It Made Me Feel
Mon			
Tue			
Wed			
Thu			
Fri			
Sat			
Sun			

After a week, review your notes. Are there patterns? Certain rooms? Emotional triggers? This tracker doesn't just identify clutter—it helps you understand its roots so you can declutter with compassion.

Mini Challenge: Declutter One Type of Clutter

Clutter shows up in different forms. This mini-challenge helps you focus on just one type: emotional, physical, or digital.

Step 1: Choose your clutter category

- Emotional: Gifts you feel guilty getting rid of
- Physical: Overflowing surfaces, drawers, closets
- Digital: Email inbox, phone photos, unused apps

Step 2: Set a timer for 15 minutes. Pick one small area. It could be your phone screen, your desk, or a box in the closet.

Step 3: Ask yourself:

- Do I still use this?
- Does this add value or stress?
- Am I holding this out of guilt or fear?

Step 4: Let go—or make a decision. Even if you don't toss anything today, clarity is a win. Understanding your hesitation is part of the work.

Encouragement to Carry Forward

Understanding clutter isn't about blaming yourself for the mess. It's about discovering the layers beneath it. When you slow down and listen to what your clutter is saying, you begin to reclaim not just space—but freedom. These tools are here to help you begin gently, with awareness and intention. Even one drawer cleared with mindfulness is a powerful step forward.

Chapter 2
THE PSYCHOLOGY OF HABITS

Do you have that feeling that you've driven home without giving a single turn any conscious thought? Your brain did all the work for you because the route was so familiar. There was no need to urge you to slow down for that sharp bend or to turn left at the light. That's how habits work. Once created, they automatically lead us through our daily lives. This technology frees up mental resources for more important tasks by operating silently in the background.

The same mechanism that makes it easier for us to tie our shoes or brush our teeth in the morning also controls how we maintain our living areas. That coat you throw on the same chair every time? On the table, that stack of unopened mail? They are also habits. These are simply ones that developed accidentally. We must comprehend this psychological structure and learn how to remodel it if we are to genuinely alter the way we organize our houses and simplify our lives.

How Habits Are Formed (Cue, Routine, Reward)

Willpower isn't the only thing that forms habits. Cue, routine, and reward are predictable neural loops that build them. The first step in creating behavior that endures is comprehending this cycle.

The trigger is called a cue. It is the cue that initiates a behavior. Environmental, emotional, and sensory cues are all possible. For instance, entering the kitchen first thing in the morning is a cue. The same goes for hearing a particular sound, seeing your shoes by the door, or even just feeling stressed or bored.

The real conduct that ensues is the routine. It is the action you take in reaction to the stimulus. Making a cup of coffee is one example of a routine in the kitchen. Snacking or browsing through your phone could be the norm if tension is the cue. Dropping your bag at the door rather than putting it away is a common habit when it comes to home clutter. It just happens; it's not an intentional choice.

The prize follows. This is the section that trains your brain to repeat the behavior and reinforces it. Big rewards are not necessary. They can be as subtle as the comfort of postponing a task or the relief you get when you finally sit down. The habit loop can be reinforced by even the slightest emotional boost.

These loops become profoundly ingrained over time. The brain learns to link the cue to the activity and the reward because it is constantly looking for ways to be more efficient. The behavior becomes increasingly automatic when the loop repeats more frequently.

This cycle applies to both beneficial and unhelpful habits. It's also a cue-routine-reward loop if you always clean the kitchen counters after brewing coffee. The visual gratification of a tidy environment could be the prize. Once this loop is identified, it can be used to develop new, helpful behaviors.

The good news is that habits can be broken. They can be modified, swapped out, and reconstructed. But in order to do it, we must comprehend their motivations. Awareness of the cue and a desire to change the reward are the first steps toward change, not the routine.

Why Decluttering Efforts Often Fail Without Habit Support

Most people take a sprint approach to decluttering. They enter a room or closet with the intention of controlling the disorder, driven by inspiration or frustration. And it works for a time. There is a surge of satisfaction when the shelves are cleared, and the bags are full. However, the clutter returns after a few weeks or months. The same corner is reached by the same pile. The chaos reappears. And despondency follows.

Because decluttering alone doesn't address the habits that first caused the clutter, this pattern keeps happening. Old patterns reappear when new habits aren't established. Although the surroundings may alter, the brain's automatic reactions don't.

Consider clearing out your foyer. You make room, install hooks, and even set up a chic mail basket. However, nothing will change in the long run if you continue to arrive, drop your bag on the floor, and throw the mail on the table. The habit isn't there, but the setting is.

This explains why so many organizing initiatives fail. People purchase containers, organize things, and design lovely systems, but they don't develop the habits necessary to keep them up to date. The processes break down in the absence of the behavioral anchor.

Habits serve as the framework for any long-term transformation. They are the silent rituals that safeguard advancement and ward off clutter on a daily basis. It is not a one-time endeavor. It concerns small, daily choices like where to put your keys, how to handle paper, and what to do with freshly laundered clothes.

We miss the real catalyst for long-lasting transformation when we ignore habit-building. Decluttering turns into a vicious cycle of short-term respite followed by unavoidable recurrence. We must slow down, focus, and begin with real-world habits if we want to end that pattern.

How to Make New Habits Stick

It's not necessary to completely change your life in order to establish enduring habits. The intention is the first step, followed by consistency. Designing small, fulfilling, and realistic habits for your present lifestyle—rather than an imagined one—is crucial.

Habit stacking is one effective strategy. This entails establishing a natural flow by joining a new habit to an already-existing one. For instance, you make coffee in the morning (an old behavior) and then spend a minute cleaning the kitchen counters (a new habit). It's simpler to incorporate the decluttering activity without resistance because your brain is already used to the coffee routine.

Visual clues are an additional technique. The formation of habits is greatly influenced by the environment. Place a visible reminder close to the door, such as a tray for keys, a sign that says "Welcome Home," or just clear away anything that causes friction if your intention is to maintain a tidy doorway. The habit is more likely to stick if it requires less mental work.

Start with absurdly small habits. The brain is more receptive to microhabits than it is to major alterations. The habit changes from "clean the living room" to "put one item back where it belongs." Rather than saying, "Declutter my desk," it says, "shred one paper." These minor victories lessen overwhelm and create momentum. Additionally, they establish a feeling of self: "I'm someone who takes care of my space."

The method still includes rewards. Positive reinforcement is necessary for the habit loop to function. Emotional benefits include a spotless surface, a peaceful time, and a cup of tea after cleaning. Don't undervalue their influence. A visual reward loop that fosters consistency is created even when you use a basic calendar or checklist to measure your progress.

More important than intensity is consistency. Five minutes a day of decluttering is more beneficial than a three-hour monthly clean-up. The brain is wired for repetition. Regular practice makes habits less willpower-intensive. They take over as the new default.

It's also critical to anticipate failures. The formation of habits is not linear. Life pauses, motivation wanes, and vitality fluctuates. Return, not perfection, is the aim. You haven't failed if you skip a day. You just stopped. Resuming guilt-free is what counts. The habit gets stronger the more quickly you return.

Accountability is beneficial. Use a journal, join a group, or tell a friend. The commitment can be strengthened just by stating the intention aloud. The process remains active in your mind thanks to shared incentives and outside reminders. When the practice is linked to self-reflection or community, you're less inclined to stray from it.

Editing old behaviors is part of developing new ones. You lessen the likelihood of reverting to the same pattern each time you eliminate a trigger for clutter, such as concealing a drop zone or removing charity goods right away. Prevention is an effective strategy. Maintaining the new habit requires less work when the surroundings encourage it.

Monitor your development, however it feels most comfortable for you. There are those who adore charts. Before-and-after pictures are taken by others. In their journals, some people write brief lines like, "Today I put away the mail right away, and it felt good." These minor compliments boost self-esteem and encourage effort. You start to believe that you are a changeable person.

Mentality is also important. Your development will be hampered if you think that developing habits is difficult or that you are not a stickler for rules. Gently challenge those ideas. As an alternative, use the phrase, "This is new, so that it will take time." "I don't have to be perfect to be consistent." "Each time I try again, I'm building something real."

The magic occurs during the identity transition. Change is more enduring when your behaviors align with the person you wish to be. Since decluttering is in line with your self-perception, you start doing it organically rather than by force. "I'm someone who values a calm home." "I take care of my space because it takes care of me."

Ultimately, habits are more about structure than willpower. They are formed by repeated decisions, influenced by your surroundings, and cemented by the significance you ascribe to them. They are foundations, not short routes. Even when motivation wanes, they support your objectives and sustain your progress.

This chapter has covered the formation of habits, their importance to effective decluttering, and strategies for maintaining them. Instead of taking huge leaps, the path to a more orderly, tranquil house is paved with small, deliberate measures that are frequently taken. The change endures once those actions become instinctive.

Make habits your silent comrades. Allow them to operate in the background, guiding you toward relaxation and clarity. You will eventually be carried farther by them than by willpower. Let's keep moving forward with the resources that enable change to be both feasible and long-lasting.

Bonus Materials

Understanding the psychology behind habits is the key to creating a home that stays tidy, not just temporarily, but for life. Below are tools you can use to shift your routines and build sustainable, clutter-free systems gently—one tiny habit at a time.

Printable Habit Tracker: Build Your Decluttering Momentum

Use this tracker to create and maintain micro-habits that keep your space in flow. You don't need to do everything at once—just commit to showing up consistently.

How to use: Pick 1–3 daily or weekly habits from the list below. Mark an X or ✔ each time you complete one. Try to build streaks—not to be perfect, but to stay present.

Week	Make Bed	Clear Kitchen Sink	5-Min Tidy	One Thing Away	Declutter One Item
Mon					
Tue					
Wed					
Thu					
Fri					
Sat					
Sun					

Optional Habits to Customize:

- Reset your desk each night
- Fluff pillows and straighten the couch
- Return all shoes to their proper place
- Set a 10-minute evening reset timer

Checklist: Habit Formation Toolkit

Use this checklist as a mental guide whenever you're trying to form a new decluttering habit. It's based on the proven habit loop: **cue →, routine →, reward.**

☐ **Choose a cue.**

Tie your habit to something you already do. Example: After brushing your teeth, wipe down the bathroom counter.

☐ **Make it obvious.**

Visual triggers help. Keep your "declutter basket" where you can see it.

☐ **Keep the routine short.**

Aim for small, achievable steps. "Tidy one drawer" is more effective than "Organize the whole room."

☐ **Reward yourself.**

Pair the habit with something enjoyable. Light a candle. Brew a cup of tea. Play a favorite playlist.

☐ **Track your streaks.**

Use the printable tracker above to stay encouraged—not pressured.

☐ **Reassess weekly.**

What's working? What feels like a drag? Adjust habits to fit your life, not the other way around.

Day Decluttering Challenge – Habit Edition

This special version of the challenge introduces one tiny habit each day. You're not just decluttering—you're training your brain to build consistency.

Day	Habit Challenge
1	Make your bed with intention. Feel the shift.
2	Set a 5-minute timer. Tidy whatever is in front of you.
3	Pick one item you no longer need. Let it go.
4	Before bed, clear one surface. Any surface.
5	Choose a "home" for your keys or bag. Always return them.
6	Create a "donation box" near your front door.
7	Write a sticky note with your new mantra: "Small wins matter."

Bringing It All Together

Habits are not about willpower—they're about design. Create an environment that makes the right choices easier, not harder. And remember: even if you miss a day, you haven't failed. You've simply paused. You can always begin again—with one small act of intention.

CREATING YOUR VISION FOR A CLEANER LIFE

Often, the moment is silent. It could strike while sitting in the midst of an untidy mess that never seems to go away or while standing at the doorway of a cluttered room. Frustration rises in waves. It goes beyond the strewn-about socks, the packed drawer, or the dishes that keep getting bigger every day. It's a feeling of being trapped. You're always struggling with your space, not simply managing it. And you know deep down that there's a better way. Simply put, you're not yet certain what that looks like.

Herein lies the role of vision. Something has to alter within before anything changes on the outside. A vision is more than a picture of a minimalist house or a Pinterest board. It is your subjective, emotionally charged vision of what your house could be and how you would like to feel there. Clarity, not perfection, is what vision is. It's not a map; it's a compass. It provides your everyday routine with a purpose and direction for your efforts. Even the most effective plans fail without it.

Finding out what a cleaner, more tranquil existence looks like for you is the focus of this chapter. Not another person. Not an influencer with boundless time and a walk-in pantry. You. Your space, your habits, your demands. This approach starts with shutting your eyes to the mess and opening your mind to what might be, regardless of how big or little your home is.

Envisioning Your Ideal Space

Everybody has a distinct ideal space. Some people see it as a warm, inviting house with sentimental objects and gentle textures. Others find it to be airy, light, and simple—a welcome change. Beneath those distinctions, however, is a common desire: convenience. There is more to the perfect space than appearance. It has to do with how it operates and how it facilitates your everyday routine, how it makes you feel less overwhelmed and more rooted.

Take a step back from your existing space to begin. Don't focus on the frustration, the to-do lists, or the disarray. Rather, ask yourself how I would feel if my home were operating flawlessly. How would the mornings be? After a long day, how would it feel to enter the room? From the time you wake up until you wind down, picture the cadence of your perfect day.

And where are things stored in your vision? How simple is it for you to locate what you need? What's hidden away, and what's on the counters? Does your home have a calm, productive, or playful atmosphere? Allow yourself to think about these concepts without passing judgment. You're establishing an aim rather than a standard.

Consider every room in your house. Your gathering place could be the kitchen. Your bedroom might turn into a haven for you. Instead of rushing, your bathroom might be a place to refresh. Imagine how each room could fulfill its function without any problems. Consider what it might be like to navigate these areas naturally rather than avoiding them.

Consider what belongs in this vision of the future. Which items fit the lifestyle you're attempting to establish? What exists because it benefits you, upholds you, or makes you happy? Which elements—those that increase anxiety, guilt, or perplexity—are missing?

It's not about escaping reality when you visualize your dream house. It involves rethinking what is feasible and providing your mind with a tangible goal to strive toward. When we have a clear vision of the future, we start taking actions that get it closer. Your daily decisions, such as where to put your shoes, how to handle the mail, and what to accept, start to fit into that bigger picture.

Identifying Pain Points and Problem Areas

Vision is more than just a dream. Being truthful about what isn't working is also important. You have to admit the friction before you can proceed. Which aspects of your house irritate you the most? Which habits make you feel resentful, overburdened, or behind?

Begin with the times when you sigh. Why can't anyone find anything in the early rush? Is it the mound that persists on the kitchen counter despite frequent clearing? Are you avoiding opening the closet in the hall? These areas are more than just disorganized. They are signals. Every area where your existing configuration fails to support your real life is a pain point.

Lack of systems, lack of space, and lack of clarity are the three main causes of pain spots. When something is unclear, you don't know what belongs where or why you're keeping it at all. Having too much stuff and not enough room might be a literal lack of space. Furthermore, a space that is neat once is not maintained due to a lack of systems.

Take the time to examine your patterns. Where do things usually accumulate? What is duplicated or lost? When you're cleaning, where do you hesitate because you're unsure of where something belongs? They are not failures. They are information. They assist you in making well-informed decisions rather than haphazard ones.

Grab a notebook and take a new look around your house. Don't feel guilty about the mess. Examine it with interest. What isn't functioning, and why? Shoes in the hallway all the time, for instance, may indicate that your storage area is too far from the entrance. Perhaps you should reconsider your folding routine or schedule if your clothes are left unfolded for days.

Take emotional pain points into account as well. Which areas make you feel exhausted? What things cause you to feel hopeless, depressed, or embarrassed? Emotional weight can be attached to clutter. Subtle but persistent resistance can be caused by a gift you didn't like, an unfinished job, or a stack of documents that makes you feel stressed. You may start prioritizing where to focus your energy by determining these hotspots.

The way forward becomes easier once the friction is readily visible. You start creating processes that genuinely function instead of attempting to clean your way out of frustration. Chaos is transformed into insight by awareness, and change is the result of understanding.

The Clean Life Vision Statement

It's time to combine everything into a single, concise statement. The Clean Life Vision Statement is neither a motivating saying nor a mission statement. It is a customized, useful statement of what you are producing and why it is important. This declaration serves as your compass, a reminder of your goals and principles.

Your true priorities should be reflected in your vision statement. It should express how you want your home to feel and how you want your room to work for you. It may emphasize comfort, tranquility, functionality, originality, or liberty. It should be brief enough to retain and significant enough to serve as a guide when your motivation wanes.

The following could be the format of a vision statement: "I am creating a home that gives me calm mornings, restful evenings, and space to focus on what matters."

Or: "My environment is a reflection of who I am becoming, not of who I was. Everything I own contributes to happiness, comfort, or meaning."

Or: "I want to enter and feel calm rather than overwhelmed. I can connect, think, and rest better at home." There is no one correct way to compose yours. The fact that it feels real is what counts. It should strike a chord with you when you read it. It should serve as a reminder of the value of the work. Additionally, this statement will assist you in getting back on track when life becomes chaotic, as it always will.

Your Clean Life Vision Statement should be kept in a prominent location. You may set it as the backdrop of your phone, put it in your planner, or frame it to hang on your wall. Let it be a silent yet effective mentor. Think about your vision if you're deciding whether to keep something, renovate a room, or persevere through a challenging endeavor. Do you think this will help the life I'm building?

The statement of your vision is dynamic. It'll change as your life changes. Your awareness of your needs and values will develop as you mature. However, the process of developing a guiding vision will never go out of style. There is no one ideal result. It's about establishing a connection with your space that respects your goals.

Everything changes when you live in accordance with a vision. Making decisions becomes simpler. Habits are more significant. Your house becomes a partner in your well-being rather than a cause of worry. The Clean Life Vision Statement is a game-changer, not just a phrase.

You have envisioned your dream space, recognized the obstacles that stand in your way, and developed a vision that aligns with your values in this chapter. These aren't merely workouts. They serve as the cornerstone for all subsequent developments. It's simple to get lost when you don't have a clear goal in mind. But you have a way if you have vision. And that route will see you through the highs and lows, the triumphs and failures, and the day-to-day effort to make your life seem lighter, more at ease, and more like your own.

Use this vision as motivation. Allow it to serve as the prism through which you choose your tools, organize your home, and form your habits. You can have the space you desire. And it's already starting to take shape, one obvious decision at a time, with patience and intention.

Section 2

DECLUTTERING FOUNDATIONS

Chapter 4

THE 5 DECLUTTERING PRINCIPLES

The drawer refused to close. It was because something had jammed behind the socks—again, not because it was broken. An individual thing that had crossed the line between order and anarchy. Does that sound familiar? It could be the hallway closet, the rubbish drawer, or that one chair that is constantly overflowing with clothing. The mess returns no matter how many times we clean it up. The reason for this is that decluttering involves more than just getting rid of things; it also involves changing the way we think about what we keep, how we use it, and what we anticipate from our space.

Decluttering is a continuous process. It's a way of thinking. It also requires a framework or a set of guiding ideas, just like any other mindset. These guidelines aid in overcoming the overwhelm and providing clarity to a sometimes emotional, perplexing, or even unachievable process. Everything starts to feel more doable when you tackle decluttering with these five concepts in mind. You're not responding to the mess anymore. You're reacting with intention.

1. Keep Only What Serves You

This idea is straightforward, yet it's not always that way. It challenges you to question yourself, "Does this serve me?" after examining every item you own. Not in the sense of "Was this expensive?" but rather "Was this a gift?" rather "Might I need this someday?" nevertheless, "Does this item support my life right now?"

Our possessions ought to be beautiful, meaningful, or helpful. That does not imply that every item must be joyful or have a profound backstory. It implies that you should occupy your space with items that directly improve or ease your life. An effective can opener. One of your favorite sweaters. A picture that brings a smile. You benefit from these things.

Things that don't help you tend to make noise. They demand attention, take up room, and need upkeep. They may bring to mind regrettable previous choices or lives you no longer lead.

Letting rid of these things is about liberation, not waste. Making space opens the door to the potential of something better.

This idea also encourages honesty. Is that treadmill collecting dust? It could be more of a monument to guilt than to fitness. Is the third bowl set for mixing? Most likely, it is not simplifying your baking. Minimizing for the sake of minimization is not the same as keeping only what is useful to you. It's about making deliberate decisions.

Would I purchase this item again today? Do I really utilize it? Does it make my life easier, happier, or more clear? Otherwise, it's acceptable to let things go.

2. Start Small to Go Big

Attempting to declutter everything at once is a mistake that most people do. Four hours later, they feel overburdened and trapped after taking everything out of every drawer and piling it on the floor. Scale is the issue, not ambition. Making decisions is the process of decluttering, and decision fatigue is a real thing.

Starting small is the best approach to achieving significant progress. Just one drawer. Just one shelf. Just one category. Your brain does not become alarmed when you concentrate on a small area. You remain involved. You experience the joy of finishing. This drive continues into the following domain. Little victories add up to big outcomes.

Starting small has psychological advantages. You gain momentum. You demonstrate to yourself that transformation is achievable. And you learn what works for your energies, your lifestyle, and your habits. You reinforce the habit each time you effectively clear out a little area. You're gaining confidence in addition to making room.

Additionally, starting modestly allows you time to become familiar with your emotional triggers. Letting go of certain things is easier than others. Your child's artwork is not the same as a junk drawer. A box of old letters is not the same as a bathroom cabinet. You provide yourself the freedom to practice without feeling rushed when you start little.

Select a location that is both accessible and visible. A counter in the kitchen. A drawer for socks. A table by the side. For fifteen minutes, set a timer. Work inside that line. Stop when the timer sounds. Have a party. Return tomorrow. One tiny, sustainable step at a time is how you go huge.

3. Think Zones, Not Rooms

When organizing, one of the most frequent errors individuals make is to tackle entire rooms without taking into account how the space is actually used. Room by room is not how real life works. Zones are where it takes place. We prepare for the day, cook, and unwind. Understanding those functional zones is crucial since these activities frequently cross over into other regions.

Thinking in zones entails concentrating on goals rather than just where you are. A "morning routine zone" could be, for instance, your kitchen counter, closet, and bathroom sink. Each of these spaces adds to a single daily routine. An example of a "work zone" might be your desk, computer drawer, and basket where you keep your laptop charger.

Your organization becomes more intuitive when you think in zones. Items are placed where they are used. Related tools are grouped together. Redundancy is eliminated. You no longer waste time moving between dispersed storage places.

Setting priorities is also aided by zone-based decluttering. Which areas are the most frictional? Which routines seem disorganized? Organizing according to function enhances the efficiency of your day. Decision weariness is lessened. You establish a setting that encourages your routines rather than undermines them.

This idea is particularly useful in communal areas. The same room may be used for several purposes by family members or roommates. Sharing becomes less stressful when zones are clearly defined and respected. You're designing it for real life, not just partitioning off space.

Determine your zones as you go through your house: cleaning, paperwork, meals, hobbies, leisure, and morning preparation. Next, pick one zone and assess it. What is effective? What isn't? What is absent? What stands in the way? Consider yourself a designer, not a housekeeper. You're designing a room that suits your needs.

4. Respect Your Future Self

You are communicating with your future self each time you make decisions about what to keep and where to store things. The decisions you make now have an impact on the version of you that will wake up tomorrow, return home exhausted, or search for scissors.

Respecting your future self entails arranging things to minimize conflict in the future. It entails not letting mistakes go in the hopes of being more driven later. It entails letting go of things that you are aware will cause you to feel guilty, frustrated, or confused in the future.

You are encouraged to act carefully by this principle. What would simplify things in the future? Next week, what would make you feel more rooted? What would make your morning more peaceful rather than chaotic?

It's simple to undervalue the impact of our surroundings on our mood in the future. A tidy foyer welcomes you in tranquility. A neat nightstand promotes better sleep. Clearer thinking is supported by a workstation that is less cluttered. These are daily presents you can give yourself, not simply pleasant bonuses.

Letting go of things that no longer represent who you are or where you're headed is another way to respect your future self. Your abandoned clothing, unfinished projects, and materials for no longer-enjoyed hobbies are all remnants of who you used to be. It's acceptable to express gratitude and go on. Five years ago, you were a different person. Nor should your space be.

According to this idea, decluttering becomes a charitable endeavor rather than a duty. Cleaning isn't all you're doing. You're fostering an atmosphere that encourages your objectives, tranquility, and vitality. Being the person you want to be is becoming easier for you.

5. Progress, Not Perfection

Progress is hampered by perfectionism. It suggests that you shouldn't do anything if you can't do everything. That your closet doesn't qualify if it doesn't resemble a picture from a magazine. Because it's not worth starting if the system isn't flawless.

However, residences are not showrooms. They are inhabited areas. They change and develop. This implies that your efforts only need to be consistent, not flawless.

This idea gives you the go-ahead to get rid of impractical aspirations. Decluttering your entire home in a single weekend is not necessary. Neither matching bins nor a label maker are required. All you have to do is begin. Then continue.

Making one drawer easier to use is progress. One corner seems more serene. One more automatic behavior. It entails appreciating the work as well as the result. Today, did you take five things out of your kitchen? That is advancement. Have your charges finally found a home? Again, progress. Every action matters.

Movement is halted by perfection. Momentum is created by progress. After a setback, you're more likely to start over if you value progress. Instead of giving up on your systems, you're more inclined to modify them. In the process, you're more likely to treat yourself with kindness.

There is no test to pass or fail when it comes to decluttering. You develop a relationship with your space. It develops over time, just like any healthy relationship. With concentration, it gets deeper. When it is founded on compassion rather than criticism, it gains greater significance.

Strive for advancement. Honor hard work. Additionally, keep in mind that it takes time to build a better home. Your daily decisions—thoughtful, honest, and imperfect—have an impact on it.

This chapter has taught you five strong decluttering tenets to guide your process. These are not only pointers. They are modes of thought. They support your habits and shape your decisions. Go back to them as you continue this task. When the path seems unclear, and the clutter seems loud, let them lead the way.

What works for you, keep it. Begin modestly. Consider zones. Honor your future self. Pay attention to the process. These are roots, not rules. Your clean life doesn't just happen when you have them. It turns into something sustainable.

Bonus Materials

The five principles in this chapter offer a powerful mindset shift—from just cleaning up to intentionally creating a home that supports your life. These bonus materials help you apply each principle with practical tools and prompts that guide you step by step.

Printable Quick-Glance Reference: The 5 Principles

Keep this visual list posted somewhere you can see it often—inside a cabinet, in your planner, or on the fridge.

The 5 Decluttering Principles:

1. **Keep only what serves you**

    (If it's not useful, beautiful, or meaningful—it's not serving.)

2. **Start small to go big.**

    (One drawer. One corner. One tiny win at a time.)

3. **Think zones, not rooms.**

    (Declutter by activity, not location—like all books, all tools, or all paperwork.)

4. **Respect your future self.**

   (What you keep today is what you'll carry tomorrow.)

5. **Progress, not perfection**

   (Messy progress beats paralyzing perfection every single time.)

Checklist: Apply the 5 Principles to Any Decluttering Task

Before you start any decluttering session, run through this list:

☐ **What zone or category am I focusing on right now?**

(Examples: kitchen tools, desk drawer, winter coats)

☐ **Is each item still serving me in this season of life?**

Ask: Do I use it? Need it? Love it? Or am I just storing it?

☐ **Am I starting with a manageable area or task?**

Resist the urge to "tackle the whole closet." Just begin with a shelf.

☐ **Will this object create a burden or relief for me in the future?**

Holding onto something "just in case" often creates more stress than peace.

☐ **Am I focusing on steady progress, not perfection?**

Give yourself credit after 15 minutes. Celebrate one drawer, not the whole dresser.

Mini Tracker: Progress, Not Perfection Log

Use this printable or notebook-based log to reinforce the principle that **showing up** matters more than finishing everything.

Date	Area You Focused On	What You Let Go	How You Felt

This tracker reinforces self-awareness and emotional progress—not just the physical changes.

30-Day Decluttering Challenge – 5 Principles Edition

This version of the challenge highlights one principle per week, helping you absorb it through small, intentional actions.

Week 1: Keep Only What Serves You

- Day 1: Look around—what item in this room do you *never* use? Let it go.
- Day 2: Remove 3 things from your closet that don't fit your current life.

- Day 3: Open your junk drawer—is anything still serving you there?

Week 2: Start Small to Go Big

- Day 8: Choose the smallest drawer in your home and declutter it.
- Day 9: Pick one shelf in the fridge—clean and organize it.
- Day 10: Spend 10 minutes tidying and stop when the timer ends.

Week 3: Think Zones, Not Rooms

- Day 15: Gather all chargers and cords in the house—sort and purge.
- Day 16: Collect all the kids' shoes in one spot—do they all still fit?
- Day 17: Tackle all cleaning supplies—expired, duplicates, or unused?

Week 4: Respect Your Future Self / Progress Not Perfection

- Day 22: Choose one item you're saving "just in case" and donate it.
- Day 23: Forgive yourself for past purchases. Let go of the guilt item.
- Day 24: Declutter one thing today—even just a broken pen.
- Day 25–30: Repeat one small action daily. Reflect on your growth.

Closing Words

These principles are tools, not rules. They aren't about doing it right—they're about doing it with *intention*. Revisit them often. Let them guide your decisions when motivation fades, and let them grow with you as your life evolves.

Chapter 5

THE DECLUTTER KICKSTART

The same choice is always made from the beginning: this is the day. The moment comes when you've stepped on the same mess too many times or when you're searching for anything basic, like a pen, a charger, or a sock, and you find yourself knee-deep in a drawer that feels like a time capsule. A garbage bag may even be in hand, along with a deep breath and a burst of motivation. The question of where to start, however, is what stops so many well-intentioned attempts.

Your solution is the Declutter Kickstart. It serves as the starting point, the warm-up, and the means of directing that motivational spark into methodical, low-pressure action. The goal of this chapter is to assist you in transitioning from intention to momentum. It allows you to avoid overwhelm, start small, and make progress quickly.

A flawless plan or a full-day purge is not necessary for decluttering. Action—simple, regular, and focused action—is the first step. You start to develop the habit of creating room for the life you desire when you take that initial step, no matter how small.

7-Day Jumpstart Plan

This is not a challenge for a makeover. This has nothing to do with remodeling your whole house in a week. The 7-Day Jumpstart is a practical, manageable method to start boosting your confidence and energy levels related to decluttering. It emphasizes little deeds that have instant benefits. The objective is to achieve short-term successes that motivate your long-term endeavors.

Focuses on a particular topic every day. 15 to 30 minutes is all you need. If it's helpful, set a timer. Play a podcast or some music. The important thing is momentum, not perfection. You can always pick up where you left off if life gets in the way. This isn't a race. A reset is taking place.

Day 1: Make the Surfaces Clear

Start with the areas that are most visible, such as desktop computers, coffee tables, nightstands, and kitchen counters. Take everything out. Make the surface clean. Restore only the items you love or use on a daily basis. Everything else either ends up in a drawer, a new home, or the door. Clear surfaces instantly convey a sense of composure and authority.

Day 2: Tidy Up Your Hallway

This is the start and finish of your day. Take out your worn-out coats, old shoes, strewn-about bags, and paper clutter. If necessary, add a basket, tray, or hanger system, but first, concentrate on removing the visual clutter. The mood of your entire room is established by your entrance.

Day 3: Clear Out a Trash Drawer

Select a drawer that has turned into a catch-all. Empty everything. Put similar objects together. Throw away anything that isn't useful. Using items you already have, such as tiny boxes, trays, or even elastic bands, make compartments. A surprising amount of peace is brought about by this easy solution.

Day 4: Take Back the Sink Area in the Bathroom

Get rid of the ten lip balms you've mysteriously accumulated, samples you'll never use, and outdated goods. Clean the surfaces. Don't keep more than you use every day. Put things in containers, bins, or drawers for convenient access. Your morning ritual has become slightly more relaxed.

Day 5: Clean the bedside table

Take out any documents, wires, empty water glasses, and novels you've finished or never begun. Turn this area into a tiny haven. Include a soothing object, such as a candle or a sentimental picture. Your rest is supported here. Make it seem that way.

Edit Your Closet Essentials on Day Six

Pick one type of apparel, such as only shirts or only shoes. Put them on if necessary. Give up things that don't fit, feel nice, or fit your way of life right now. Make one area of the closet more functional rather than organizing the entire thing. Mornings can be quicker and less stressful with minor wardrobe adjustments.

Day 7: Get Rid of One Paper Stow

Pick up a tiny stack of paper from your most vexing pile, such as forms, mail, or receipts. Recycle anything that isn't needed. Save the important things. Shred anything delicate. Only one pile. That's all. It feels like progress to have even one folder of clarity. This helps you become more confident in your ability to make decisions, which is crucial for dealing with larger heaps in the future.

Every one of these tasks is intended to yield a rapid victory. Not only will you have more room at the end of the week, but you'll also have a better understanding of your routines, habits, and the most important things in your house. Additionally, it helps you discover your own rhythm for decluttering. Some people enjoy beginning with simple victories. Some people like a challenge. You can find what works for you with the help of this plan.

Declutter Checklist by Category

Hidden clutter can be found in many different areas of every home. Not everything is clear. While some are hidden in plain sight, others are buried in cupboards. The most typical clutter categories are broken down in this checklist, along with detailed instructions on what to look for in each. It should be used as a guide, not a manual. You don't need to finish everything at once. Select a category. Just one drawer. Just one shelf. That's where to start.

Clothing

- Clothes that don't fit, flatter, or feel like you anymore
- Single socks or damaged items you've meant to repair
- Shoes you never wear or that hurt your feet
- Accessories you haven't used in over a year
- Outdated formalwear or seasonal clothes you haven't touched in years

Papers

- Old bills, receipts, and expired warranties
- Unused notebooks, random sticky notes, and scraps
- Outdated instruction manuals and menus
- School papers or junk mail you've kept "just in case."
- Printouts from events, lists, or flyers long past their usefulness

Kitchenware

- Duplicate utensils or gadgets you never use
- Chipped mugs, lidless containers, or pans past their prime
- Spices expired over a year ago
- Plastic containers without matching lids
- That specialty tool you used once and forgot you even owned

Bathroom Products

- Expired medications and products
- Makeup you no longer use or need
- Dried-up nail polish, old razors, hotel toiletries
- Samples you've been saving "for later."
- Multiple versions of the same product "just in case."

Books and Media

- Books you've read and won't revisit
- DVDs, CDs, or games without working devices to play them
- Instructional books or manuals you've outgrown
- Duplicates or impulse buys with no emotional attachment
- Outdated textbooks and old magazines "you might read someday."

Toys and Kids' Items

- Broken toys or puzzles missing pieces
- Items your kids have outgrown or forgotten
- Games or crafts no one enjoys anymore
- Clothing that's too small or worn out
- Trinkets from party favors and fast food meals that gather dust

Decor and Seasonal

- Holiday decor you didn't use last season
- Decorative items that no longer match your style
- Gifts you kept out of guilt rather than joy
- Extras stored out of sight, out of mind
- Trendy decor that felt right once but now feels like visual clutter

Digital Clutter

- Unused apps on your phone or tablet
- Old screenshots, blurry photos, duplicate files
- Emails you'll never need again
- Outdated documents and downloads
- Social media accounts or subscriptions you no longer enjoy

Each of these categories offers a starting point. Some will be easier than others. That's okay. Choose based on your energy and availability. Keep a box or bag for donations nearby. Have a trash bag or recycling bin on hand. Decluttering doesn't require drama. It just needs steady movement in the right direction.

Quick Wins for Early Momentum

Momentum is more important than technique when you're just starting off. The ideal plan is not necessary. To demonstrate that development is achievable, you need a minor victory. Quick wins are useful in this situation.

Tasks that have a noticeable or emotional impact and can be completed in ten to twenty minutes are known as quick wins. You can immediately notice the changes—areas that breathe more easily, drawers that open smoothly, and routines that go more smoothly. These are crucial, particularly when time is limited or motivation is low.

Consider these quick wins:

Make a Level Surface Clear

A dining table, kitchen counter, or shelf in the foyer. Just what belongs there should be returned after cleaning and wiping it down. Just the contrast in appearance can be invigorating. An entire room's tone can be altered by just one empty area.

Take Care of the Trash

Using a bag, visit each room and gather any noticeable waste, such as broken or expired products or empty packaging. Just disposal, no decisions. The sensation of lightness that comes from just getting rid of garbage will astound you.

Clear out the car by getting rid of stray toys, empty water bottles, old receipts, and neglected workout attire. If you have time, vacuum. You just had a lighter commute. Your daily commute is more peaceful when your automobile is clean.

Make a Box for Donations

Place it somewhere people can see it. Drop things in as you go about your day. Arrange for a pickup or drop-off when it's full. This box becomes a living component of the rhythm of your house and a representation of continuous development.

Clear out the clutter. Your Backpack or Purse.

Drain it entirely. Take out everything that doesn't belong, such as trash or outdated receipts. Repack just the necessities. No matter where you travel, you'll have greater clarity.

Delete and unsubscribe

Take five minutes to unsubscribe from newsletters you never read and delete emails you don't want to receive. Digital clarity is also important. You should guard your focus.

Consolidate Cleaning Supplies Sort items according to their type. Throw away empty bottles. Keep in a single, easily accessible location. Organize your supplies to make cleaning easy. Streamlining tools makes the work seem less intimidating.

Additionally, you can create your own fast victories. Perhaps it's throwing out the rest and wearing matching socks. Perhaps it's only clearing off one shelf in your refrigerator. The act of showing up, making room, and developing the conviction that you're moving forward is more important than the activity itself.

In the beginning, it's more important that you do something than how much you do. Motion is produced by even the slightest change. And that movement results in increased energy, clarity, and motivation to keep going.

You have entered the actual realm of action in this chapter. You've studied the 7-day kickstart plan, gone over the most typical clutter categories, and gathered suggestions for easy victories that will help you get started. The purpose of these tools is to assist you in creating early successes. Movement is important, not because perfection is the aim.

Eliminating everything isn't the goal of decluttering. It's about creating space for the important things. Starting with one drawer, one shelf, or one tiny step at a time is the greatest way to get started. Your subsequent steps feel simpler when your initial step is light. Momentum takes over. And the mess begins to go away, not just from your house but also from your thoughts.

This is the beginning of your journey. Allow it to guide you into the next stage of your more tranquil, clean life.

Bonus Materials

Starting is often the hardest part. This chapter helps you move from intention into action—without overwhelm. The tools below are designed to make that first step feel lighter, more focused, and even a little bit more fun.

Printable 7-Day Jumpstart Plan

This beginner-friendly plan gives you one clear, manageable task per day. Each activity builds momentum while reinforcing trust in your ability to keep going.

Day	Declutter Focus	Action
1	**Visible Surfaces**	Clear one tabletop—desk, coffee table, or dresser. Keep only what you love or use daily.
2	**The Catch-All Drawer**	Tackle one junk drawer. Dump it out. Toss what doesn't serve. Re-home the rest.
3	**Clothing You No Longer Wear**	Fill a grocery bag with items you haven't worn in a year. Donate it today.
4	**Bathroom Declutter**	Toss expired products, samples, and broken tools. Wipe drawers.
5	**Paper Clutter**	Sort a single stack—mail, bills, kids' art. Keep what matters. Recycle the rest.
6	**Kitchen Counter Clarity**	Remove all non-daily-use items. Put back only the essentials. Breathe.
7	**Celebrate & Reflect**	Walk your home. Acknowledge what you did. Write down what felt easiest—and what helped.

Print it. Post it. Mark off each day as you complete it. Visual progress builds momentum.

Category-by-Category Declutter Checklist

This cheat sheet helps you see clutter in terms of categories—not rooms. Use it as a master reference as you progress.

☐ **Clothes** – Items you don't wear, don't fit, or make you feel "meh."

☐ **Shoes** – Uncomfortable, worn out, or never used

☐ **Papers** – Old receipts, junk mail, manuals, duplicate files

☐ **Books** – Never-read novels, outdated textbooks, duplicates

☐ **Kitchenware** – Broken utensils, single-purpose gadgets, excess mugs

☐ **Pantry** – Expired goods, old spices, food you'll never eat

☐ **Toiletries** – Expired creams, half-used samples, duplicates

☐ **Toys** – Broken pieces, outgrown games, loud annoyances

☐ **Office Supplies** – Dried pens, random cords, cluttered drawers

☐ **Linens** – Stained towels, threadbare sheets, excess duplicates

☐ **Decor** – Dust collectors, unused frames, old candles

☐ **Electronics** – Broken devices, unused cables, extra remotes

Don't try to tackle all of these at once. Choose one category at a time. Give yourself permission to go slow.

Quick Wins List: Small Areas, Big Impact

These are the most satisfying mini-projects when you're short on time but craving a visual win.

- **Purse or Backpack:** Empty it out, toss trash, restock only essentials
- **One Shelf in the Fridge:** Wipe it down, toss expired leftovers
- **Shoe Rack or Mat:** Pair shoes, remove extras, vacuum or wipe
- **Car Glove Compartment:** Remove outdated papers, stock napkins
- **Top of the Dresser:** Clear, dust, and replace only intentional items
- **Nightstand Drawer:** Toss random cords, wrappers, expired meds

Each of these tasks takes 5–15 minutes. They're perfect for jumpstarting a day—or rescuing a messy week.

Mini 7-Day Habit Tracker: Build Your Decluttering Streak

Use this to track momentum during your Kickstart week.

Day	I Decluttered Something	How I Felt Afterwards
1		
2		
3		
4		
5		
6		
7		

This isn't about pressure—it's about progress. One drawer a day keeps the chaos away.

Chapter 6

LETTING GO WITHOUT GUILT

The box had been taped shut for years. It moved from one apartment to the next, untouched but never discarded. Inside were things once deemed important—college notebooks, greeting cards, mismatched trinkets. Opening it wasn't easy. Not because it was heavy but because of what it represented. A version of life once lived. Moments long passed. People are no longer present. Sorting through it felt like a betrayal as if letting go meant forgetting. The truth, however, is something gentler: letting go is not forgetting—it's choosing to live lighter.

Guilt is one of the strongest emotional barriers to decluttering. It whispers that we're wasteful, ungrateful, and disloyal. It attaches itself to memories, relationships, and our sense of identity. But holding onto items out of guilt doesn't preserve the past—it burdens the present. This chapter is about releasing that burden. Not by discarding carelessly but by letting go with understanding, compassion, and intention.

Emotional Attachments to Objects

Our homes are filled with more than things—they're filled with meaning. A ticket stub from a concert years ago. A scarf from a trip abroad. A chipped mug from college. These aren't just objects; they're vessels of emotion. They carry memories, identities, and moments that matter.

That's why decluttering isn't just physical work. It's emotional work. Letting go can feel like erasing a part of your story. You might hesitate at a shirt you haven't worn in years because it reminds you of who you were when you wore it. You might hold onto a kitchen gadget because it represents the person you hoped to become.

Emotional attachment is not the enemy. It's a sign that you've lived, loved, experienced. But when every item becomes sacred, your space becomes a museum—not a home. There's a difference between honoring your life and hauling its weight into every corner of your current one.

Start by noticing your reaction. When you hold something and feel resistance to letting it go, ask why. What does it represent? What emotion comes up? Sometimes naming it—joy, sadness, guilt, fear—gives you the clarity to decide whether the object is still serving you.

You can thank the item for the role it played in your life. Gratitude is a powerful step in the release process. Say, "Thank you for being part of this chapter." Then, allow yourself to part with it, knowing the value of the moment stays with you, even if the item does not.

The truth is, some objects are placeholders for things we wish we still had—time, youth, a former version of ourselves. Letting go can feel like surrendering that part of life. But what if you reframed it as making space for who you're becoming?

One helpful tool is to keep a memory box. A small container where truly meaningful items can live without overwhelming your space. When everything is special, nothing is. But when you choose intentionally, your memory box becomes a curated collection of your most treasured pieces—not a dumping ground of indecision.

You can also practice storytelling. If an item feels hard to part with, take five minutes to write down its story. What did it mean to you? When was it important? This exercise honors the memory while giving you freedom from the object. You're preserving the emotion, not the clutter.

Gifts, Heirlooms, and "Just in Case" Items

Few items carry more emotional weight than gifts and heirlooms. These are things we didn't choose, but they feel heavy and obligation-inducing. A sweater gifted from a distant relative. A decorative bowl passed down from a grandparent. A figurine from a friend's vacation. Even if you don't like the item, even if it clashes with your style, there's guilt woven into every glance.

But here's the truth: a gift's purpose is to bring joy to the receiver. Once given, it belongs to you. You are not required to keep something forever simply because it was a present. If it doesn't serve your life or suit your home, it's okay to let it go. The love, the gesture, the thoughtfulness—they've already done their work.

Heirlooms can be even trickier. They carry family history, personal legacy, and cultural significance. But not every heirloom must live in your home to be honored. Ask yourself: does this item bring you joy, connection, or beauty? Or does it live in a box, untouched and unappreciated?

You might choose to keep heirlooms that truly resonate. You might take photos of others before passing them on. You might offer them to family members who would value them more. Respect for history doesn't mean bearing its weight in your home. History can be honored in many ways: through storytelling, shared memories, or preservation in a more fitting place.

If you struggle with letting go of a gift, remind yourself that the person who gave it to you likely wanted your happiness. Would they want you to feel burdened by it? If the answer is no, then you have permission to release it.

Then there are the "just in case" items. These are future-based fears disguised as practicality. The broken toaster you might fix. The extra curtains you might need. The stacks of old tech cables, outdated manuals, expired coupons. These items are rarely missed when they're gone. But they occupy prime real estate in your space and your mental load.

Letting go of "just in case" items requires trust. Trust that if you truly need it again, you'll find a solution. Trust that your space and peace of mind are more valuable than hypothetical scenarios. Trust that what you need most often is already within reach, not buried under what-ifs.

A helpful practice is to set a boundary. Designate a small box or shelf as your "just in case" zone. When it fills up, review and reassess. If something hasn't been touched since the last check-in, let it go. This adds structure to what can otherwise become an excuse for indefinite accumulation.

You can also practice the 20/20 rule: if it costs less than $20 and can be replaced in less than 20 minutes, it doesn't need to be stored indefinitely. This small boundary can help loosen the grip of "just in case" fear and make room for peace and clarity.

Try asking yourself: when was the last time I used this? If it's been a year—or more—it's probably safe to let go. If the item is inexpensive and easily replaceable, release it. Holding onto fear creates clutter. Trusting yourself creates space.

Reframing Value and Memory

Value is often mistaken for cost. We think, "But I paid good money for this," or "This was expensive," and use that to justify keeping something we no longer use. But the true value isn't found in price tags. It's found in purpose.

If something is costing you space, stress, or decision fatigue, it's not adding value—it's draining it. The money has already been spent. Keeping the item won't bring it back. Letting go isn't wasteful. It's wise. It's recognizing that your current needs are more important than sunk costs.

You can also reframe memory. Instead of asking, "What does this item help me remember?" ask, "What do I remember without this item?" If the memory is strong, the item isn't necessary. And if the memory has faded, perhaps the item isn't serving you as much as you think.

Photos, voice notes, or written reflections can all serve as substitutes for bulky physical items. You don't need to keep every childhood drawing to remember your child's creativity. You don't need every souvenir to cherish the trip. Pick one or two items that best represent the memory—and let the rest go.

Reframing also applies to identity. You are not your possessions. You are not the books you never finished, the projects you abandoned, the clothing sizes you've grown out of. You are a dynamic, evolving person. Your space should reflect who you are now—not who you were five years ago.

The best question you can ask yourself is: does this support the person I am becoming? If not, let it go. Release the guilt, the story, the weight. Honor your past. But live in the present.

Letting go without guilt is an act of self-respect. It's not rejection. It's release. It's saying, "I choose space over shame. Clarity over clutter. Intention over obligation."

Letting go might feel difficult in the moment, but freedom comes afterward. You'll begin to notice that the space in your home feels different—lighter, calmer. And you'll realize that what remains are the things that matter most.

In this chapter, we explored the emotional roots of guilt tied to objects. We unpacked the challenge of gifts, heirlooms, and just-in-case items. We examined how to reframe value and memory in ways that support forward movement. Each item you release is not a loss. It's a step toward living with more ease, more intention, and more freedom.

Your home has not been a storage unit for the past. It's a sanctuary for your life today. And the space you make by letting go is space you reclaim for peace, presence, and possibility.

Keep the lessons. Keep the love. Let go of the rest.

You are not discarding your story. You're creating a cleaner chapter—one that reflects who you are now and welcomes who you're becoming.

Section 3

BUILDING DAILY ORGANIZATION HABITS

Chapter 7
DAILY CLEAN HABITS FOR EVERY ROOM

The kitchen counter was softly illuminated by the morning sun that came in through the window. Or it ought to have, anyway. Mail, keys, an empty coffee mug, yesterday's lunch container, and a notepad that had long since outlived its usefulness were all in the way of the light. What ought to have been a tidy, welcoming beginning to the day seemed burdensome. And the kitchen wasn't the only place that felt heavy. It went. It carried over into the car, the bathroom, the bedroom, and even the office. A cluttered head was the result of a cluttered morning. All from a single, unnoticed surface.

The majority of individuals don't require their homes to be flawless. However, everyone wants their room to have a rhythm and feel like a place of relaxation. Sterile does not equate to clean. It means breathable, cozy, and practical. A big organizing marathon or a thorough cleaning every weekend aren't the keys to creating that kind of space. The little routines you follow on a daily basis, the tasks that take ten minutes or less are what make your house work for you rather than against you.

This chapter looks at how to create doable, everyday routines that subtly uphold order without becoming overbearing. These behaviors are adaptable and understanding. They don't need strict procedures or perfection. Rather, they assist you in incorporating calm, clarity, and ease into each room of your house.

10-Minute Daily Habits by Room

Any room can benefit from a few deliberate behaviors, regardless of the size of your house or the structure of your day. These aren't comprehensive cleaning procedures. These are upkeep activities that prevent clutter and lessen the need for later, more involved cleaning tasks.

Kitchen

- Wipe down the counters after each meal. Even if it's just a damp cloth swipe, the clear surface resets the space.

- Load or unload the dishwasher right away. Don't let dishes "soak" for days. A five-minute rinse is easier than a hardened scrub.
- Toss expired leftovers each morning. One glance at the fridge can prevent mystery odors and wasted space.
- Keep a clean sink. Train your eyes to feel relaxed when there's no pile-up. If it takes under two minutes, do it now.

Living Room

- Do a quick floor check at the end of the day. Shoes, toys, mail, or dishes—scoop them up in one round.
- Fluff and reposition pillows and blankets. It creates an instant sense of care.
- Clear the coffee table or side tables. They tend to collect mail, magazines, and cups. Resetting them visually changes the whole room.

Bathroom

- Wipe the sink after brushing your teeth. A simple rinse and swipe prevents buildup.
- Hang towels properly to dry. It keeps the room fresh and less musty.
- Return products to drawers or bins instead of leaving them out. Less visual clutter equals a calmer start to your day.

Bedroom

- Make the bed each morning. It takes less than three minutes and sets a tone of readiness.
- Empty your pockets and declutter your nightstand before bed.
- Use a laundry basket daily. Don't let clothes land on the floor or a chair. Train yourself to put them away or in the hamper right away.

Entryway

- Reset this area every evening. Return shoes, hang coats, and clear off the console or table.
- Have a designated space for keys, bags, and mail. Don't just drop them anywhere. This habit prevents clutter from entering the rest of your home.

Home Office or Workspace

- Tidy the desk at the end of each workday. Put away supplies, stack papers neatly, and close tabs or programs you're done with.

- Review your to-do list or notes for the next day. This habit closes the mental loop and allows you to transition into personal time more peacefully.

Each of these habits takes just a few minutes, but they act like anchors. They keep your environment steady even on busy days. They add up to a space that feels intentional and cared for.

Morning vs. Evening Reset Routines

Resets are not about cleaning everything. They're about bringing space back to neutral—a baseline of calm and functionality. The best way to do this is by sandwiching your day with simple morning and evening resets.

Morning Reset

Your morning reset is a signal to start fresh. It doesn't have to be long or detailed. Even five minutes can make a big impact.

- Make the bed. It's a visual win and a signal to your brain that the day is beginning.
- Open curtains or blinds. Letting light in resets your internal rhythm and makes the space feel more alive.
- Do a quick bathroom tidy. Wipe the sink, replace towels, and check the toilet paper stash.
- Put away any dishes left drying overnight. Starting with clear counters and a clean sink feels energizing.

You can make your morning reset part of your coffee or tea routine. While the water boils or the coffee brews, take a few moments to breathe life into your space. This transition between rest and activity sets the tone for your day.

Evening Reset

The evening reset is a gift to your future self. It's your way of saying, "I've got your back tomorrow."

- Clear the kitchen counters. Even if dinner dishes aren't all done, remove clutter from the surfaces.
- Do a 10-minute family tidy-up. Everyone grabs a bin or basket and returns items to their home.
- Prep one small thing for the next day—lay out clothes, make a to-do list, fill the coffee pot.

- Turn off overhead lights and switch to soft lighting or lamps. This cues your body that it's time to slow down.

Avoiding making the reset a chore is crucial. It ought to resemble a wind-down custom. To add enjoyment to the occasion, use aromatherapy, music, or low lighting. Eventually, it stops being a chore and instead becomes a soothing way to end the day.

Start with one room if you've never done a reset before. When it's dirty, pick the spot that stresses you off the most. This is frequently the living room or kitchen. Make it the focus of a five-minute routine. Expand to additional areas after that becomes second nature.

The Power of Visible Surfaces

There is a way to improve the organization of your home rapidly, and it has nothing to do with pricey containers or color-coded systems. It's this: maintain a clear surface area.

Visual magnets include desks, dressers, nightstands, counters, tables, and even the tops of appliances. Your brain remains attentive when these areas are cluttered. It perceives visual noise, decisions that need to be made, and incomplete activities.

Surfaces that are clear are peaceful. They give the mind space to breathe. They also speed up and simplify cleaning. A clear counter can be cleaned in a matter of seconds. Cleaning around objects is work and can be discouraging.

Begin modestly. Choose one surface to maintain constant clarity. Make a commitment to it. It might be your kitchen counter or dining table. You will begin to want that serene image in different contexts once you become accustomed to it.

Make sure the organism is enclosed if it must dwell on a surface. To keep small items organized, use bowls, trays, or baskets. Grouping prevents the space from appearing disorganized and provides visual respite to the brain.

Keep in mind that surfaces are not used for storing. They are breathing spaces, display rooms, and work zones. Your whole house feels more useful when you use them purposefully.

Instruct your family on this idea as well. Children can learn how to tidy their toy tables or desks. The fact that the dining table isn't a permanent mail station can be explained to partners. Respect for space is reinforced by this common philosophy.

The practice of cleaning surfaces eventually becomes second nature. Unconsciously, you move a side table as you pass it. Before it accumulates, you notice clutter beginning to accumulate and make necessary corrections. It's these little movements that prevent your space from becoming chaotic.

Also, beauty is invited by clear surfaces. A lit candle, a framed picture, or a single flower all glow in an area that isn't vying for attention. You start to see your house once more, not just the contents.

Every area in your house can be transformed with easy, everyday acts, as you have learned in this chapter. You've looked at 10-minute routines that work with actual schedules. The ability of morning and evening resets to center your day has been demonstrated to you. Additionally, you've discovered the subtle enchantment of transparent, observable surfaces.

These aren't guidelines. They are rhythms. They are not required to be flawless. All they have to do is be reliable. Your home feels different after a few minutes here and a few decisions there. Not only is it calmer, but it's cleaner. More alive, not just cleaner.

The goal of daily clean habits is not to do more. They focus on taking care of the important things in a gentle, consistent, and considerate manner because everything else goes a little more smoothly when your environment supports your life.

Allow your habits to assist you. Give your rooms some air. Allow your routines to help you regain your equilibrium. That is the main goal of daily clean life.

You'll start to learn how to expand on these routines in the upcoming chapters by implementing methods that make anything from digital clutter to laundry easier. For now, though, take a moment to appreciate this change: one tiny habit at a time, your home will become more supportive. And there is the true power of clean living above everything else.

Bonus Materials

This chapter is about turning cleanliness into a lifestyle, not a chore list. Below, you'll find supportive tools to help make those small, daily habits automatic—and maybe even enjoyable. The goal isn't perfection. It's a peaceful flow.

Printable Room-by-Room Daily Habits Chart

Use this visual as a gentle guide. Post it in a common area or keep a copy in your planner. Check off what feels doable—and give yourself grace when it doesn't.

Room	Morning Habit	Evening Habit	1-Minute Reset Tip

Bedroom	Make the bed	Place clothes in the hamper	Fluff pillows, straighten blankets
Kitchen	Empty dish rack/dishwasher	Wipe counters, clear sink	Toss food scraps, restock paper towels
Living Room	Open blinds, reset couch pillows	Return remotes and books to place	Quick surface dust with a microfiber
Bathroom	Wipe sink after use	Refill toilet paper, empty trash	Spray mirror, tidy countertop
Entryway	Put away shoes/bags	Sort mail or recycle junk mail	Sweep or shake the mat
Office	Power on the system / clear desk	Organize pens and stack papers neatly	Clear coffee mug, close browser tabs

Remember: if it takes less than a minute, do it now. These tiny resets add up.

Checklist: 10-Minute Clean Habits by Room

Perfect for days when you feel overwhelmed. Set a timer and complete just one room. Walk away with a win.

☐ **Bedroom:**

- Make bed
- Put away stray clothes
- Dust nightstand

☐ **Kitchen:**

- Unload dishwasher
- Wipe stove and sink
- Toss expired food

☐ **Bathroom:**

- Clean mirror
- Wipe the toilet seat and sink
- Replace hand towel

☐ **Living Room:**

- Reset pillows/blankets
- Stack or shelve books

- Vacuum or sweep high-traffic area

☐ **Entryway:**

- Put shoes in place
- Hang coats/bags
- Toss old mail

Customize the checklist by picking just *three actions* each day. Rotate what matters most.

Daily Clean Habit Tracker (Printable)

Track one small clean habit per day for 30 days. You don't need to do everything. You just need to stay in rhythm.

Day	Habit You Completed	Mood After Cleaning
1		
2		
3		
...		
30		

Use the "Mood" column to notice which habits most positively affect your day. Lean into those.

Mini Reset Rituals to Try Today

Sometimes, you don't have an hour—or even 20 minutes. These resets are less about time and more about *attention*.

- **One Surface, One Song:** Play a short song and reset one flat surface (desk, counter, side table).
- **Clothes Sweep:** Walk through your home and collect every stray sock, shirt, or scarf.
- **Nightstand Reset:** Toss old tissues, empty mugs, wrangle cords.
- **Light & Air Ritual:** Open a window. Light a candle. Let the space shift with breath and scent.

SYSTEMS THAT SIMPLIFY

Once more, the drawer refused to close. It was back to overflowing in a matter of days, regardless of how many times the contents were reorganized. Cables, coupons, pens, and batteries. It felt more like a trap than the junk drawer it was intended to be. The problem with clutter is that it bounces back rather than simply building up. Again and again. Unless there is a change at the bottom.

Being organized is more than just cleaning up once. It has to do with developing systems. A system is a procedure that may be repeated. It eliminates uncertainty. The turmoil is eliminated. It makes your house run more smoothly and with less effort. Everything needs energy in the absence of systems. Your space starts to function when you implement systems.

Systems that simplify, not complicate, are the focus of this chapter. The rules of home organization are applicable whether you live in a large house or a small apartment. You regain your mental capacity, save time, and lessen stress when you put even a few basic systems in place. The foundation of sustainable simplicity is systems.

Home Organization Principles (Like "A Place for Everything")

One timeless principle of house organizing is to have a place for everything and to put everything in its proper place. Although it may seem archaic, it is the foundation of any successful system. Things float if they have no home. They fall into arbitrary locations, accumulate, and become clutter.

You stop wasting time looking when everything has a place. You don't have to ponder where to place anything because it's already decided. Additionally, you don't have to make the same choice twice. The magic of systems is that they allow you to focus on other things.

Making a place for things doesn't have to be perfect. It entails being considerate. Where do you instinctively grab scissors? Where do you drop your keys every time? Instead of building your system on an impractical goal, build it around your behaviors. Systems work best when they complement your behavior rather than trying to alter it.

Begin by taking a new look around your house. Determine the areas where clutter tends to accumulate. Counters, entry tables, and bedroom nooks. Do the things here have a specific place to go? If not, designate one. Does that housework if they do? Perhaps it's not in the proper place if it's not being used.

"Like with like" is another principle that promotes efficient systems. Put comparable things in groups. Keep office supplies in a single drawer rather than five. Put all of the lightbulbs in one container. Place every medication in a single cabinet. Sorting objects into groups helps you see what you have and minimizes duplication. Additionally, this idea increases the efficiency of shopping. Knowing what you already own reduces the likelihood that you will overspend.

Another organizing principle that makes things simpler is visibility. You won't utilize it if you can't see it. Clear drawer organizers, open shelves, or transparent bins can have a profound impact. If something isn't buried in a black hole of storage, you're less likely to forget it. Consider it your home's inventory: you can use what you can see.

Finally, work on one-in, one-out. Take something old out of your house when you add something new. This avoids progressive development and maintains the equilibrium of your systems. It also compels people to make more deliberate choices. You will be more thoughtful while purchasing or retaining things if you are aware that something must go to create room.

Containers, Labels, and Flow

There is more to containers than meets the eye. They are useful instruments that assist your systems. A container serves as a delineation. It establishes the boundaries of space. It reads, "This is where this goes, and this is how much of it I'll keep."

Prioritize function overlook when selecting containers. What do you have stored? Where will it reside? How frequently will people access it? Open bins or baskets work best for products that are used frequently. Lidded boxes or stackable containers are good options for infrequent use. Remember accessibility. The method won't work if you have to shuffle five boxes to get to something.

Do not purchase too many containers before sorting. First, declutter; next, measure; and last, buy. If you don't, you'll wind up attempting to fit your belongings into the incorrect solution, or worse, creating even more mess. Beautiful baskets and bins can easily thrill you, but the container should be driven by your space rather than the other way around.

Labels make things more clear. They remove the burden of guesswork from the mind. Labels provide a mental shortcut, even if you live alone and are aware of what's inside. They promote consistency as well. You're more likely to return items to a bin labeled "First Aid" and to locate them promptly in an emergency.

A sophisticated label maker is not necessary. A marker and masking tape work perfectly. Use chalkboard tags or print personalized labels if you're a design enthusiast. Communication, not perfection, is the aim. In households, labeling also fosters common understanding. It facilitates participation from others in maintaining an orderly home.

Consider "flow"—the movement of objects within your house. Shoes, backpacks, groceries, laundry, and mail. All things have a path. Flow-supporting systems facilitate daily living.

Does the mail, for instance, end up on the counter and then get lost among receipts and keys when you bring it in? Or does it get sorted once a day and placed in a tray marked "To Review"? Could you put a shredder or a little coupon bin close by?

Another good example is laundry. Every room has a basket, right? Is it easy for filthy laundry to find its way to the washer? Because there is no established method for putting away clean clothes, do they end up piled on a chair? The entire procedure is made simpler by designating specific areas for folding, sorting, and storing laundry.

Create your systems according to your innate routines. Don't fight it if backpacks are dropped by the door; instead, place hooks or a cubby there. Place a basket close by if shoes gather at the base of the stairs. Systems that work well meet you where you are.

Flow is applicable to activities as well. Things need to be in the correct place at the right time for bedtime, cooking, morning rituals, and working from home. Your life feels more seamless when your house facilitates these everyday routines. You don't waste time retracing, hunting, or shuffling.

Maintenance vs Overhauls

One of the biggest mistakes people make in home organization is waiting until things fall apart before addressing them. Then they spend hours—sometimes days—overhauling their space, only for it to fall into disarray again. What's missing? Maintenance.

Maintenance is the quiet hero of a well-run home. It's the small, regular adjustments that keep things in order. It prevents messes from becoming monsters. It's not exciting, but it's effective. Maintenance is your everyday partner—always working in the background.

Overhauls have their place. Sometimes, a system needs a total reset. A deep clean, a major declutter, a structural change. But these should be the exception, not the rule. Overhauls take time and energy. Maintenance preserves your time by minimizing the need for deep intervention.

Build maintenance into your routine. Set a weekly "reset hour" to walk through your systems. Are bins overflowing? Are labels still accurate? Are things drifting from their homes? Quick check-ins keep your systems functional and relevant. You can also set monthly or seasonal reviews for more involved tweaks.

Maintenance also means updating your systems as life changes. With a new job, new schedule, growing kids, and seasonal routines, your systems should adapt. What worked six months ago might need tweaking now. Change isn't a failure. It's evolution.

Use visual cues to remind you. If you see clutter returning, that's a sign something isn't working. Don't wait until it overwhelms you. Adjust early and often. Your space is alive. It shifts with your lifestyle, and your systems should, too.

Another key to maintenance is delegation. Share responsibility. Systems should be simple enough that everyone in the household can follow them. Kids can return toys to labeled bins. Partners can sort mail into trays. Households run better when systems aren't dependent on one person doing it all.

Remember: perfection isn't the goal. Consistency is. Maintenance isn't about having an Instagram-ready pantry every day. It's about being able to find what you need when you need it, without stress. Systems that work for your lifestyle are the ones that last.

Systems simplify. That's their entire purpose. They're not about aesthetic displays or rigid rules. They're about making your daily life smoother, quieter, and easier. They're about creating an environment where your energy is spent on what matters—not on chaos.

In this chapter, you've explored how systems form the foundation of a well-functioning home. From the timeless principle of "a place for everything" to the practical power of containers and flow to the quiet strength of maintenance over overhaul—each piece plays a role in simplifying your space.

The organization isn't about stuff. It's about systems. And the best systems are the ones that make your home feel lighter, calmer, and easier to live in.

When your home runs on systems, life flows better. You don't need to be more disciplined—you just need better support. That's the real secret of cleaner living. You're not working harder. You're working smarter. And that makes all the difference.

Bonus Materials

This chapter is all about building systems that work *for* you—not systems that you constantly work to maintain. Below are tools to help you set up simplified systems that reduce mental load, save time, and make staying organized feel natural.

Printable Systems Setup Checklist

Use this master checklist as you walk through your space and assess where systems are missing—or too complicated.

☐ **Entryway:**

- Shoe basket or rack in place
- Hooks or designated wall space for bags/coats
- Drop zone for keys and daily items
- Small trash bin for junk mail

☐ **Kitchen:**

- Everyday items within arm's reach
- "Zone" system (prep, cook, clean, serve) established
- Pantry grouped by category (baking, snacks, cans, etc.)
- The fridge was purged and organized weekly

☐ **Bathroom:**

- One container per category (hair, skin, first aid, etc.)
- Extras stored in labeled bins or baskets
- Trash can emptied every 2–3 days

☐ **Office / Workspace:**

- Inbox tray for papers to sort
- Drawer organizers for cords, clips, pens
- Active projects stored separately from long-term files

☐ Closet / Dresser:

- Like-items grouped together (tops, bottoms, shoes)
- "One in, one out" rule posted or practiced
- Seasonal rotation system in place

☐ Laundry / Cleaning Supplies:

- Clearly labeled bins for light/dark/hand-wash
- Small caddy or basket for each type of cleaning supply
- Quick checklist for reordering essentials

Print and post this checklist to use over time—no need to do it all at once!

Container & Labeling Guide: Simplify Your Storage

Best Container Choices:

- Clear bins for visibility (especially in pantries and craft areas)
- Soft baskets for living rooms and bedrooms (toys, throws, books)
- Stackable boxes for closets and seasonal storage
- Divided trays for drawers (bathroom, office, kitchen)

Smart Labeling Tips:

- Use simple, readable language
- Add emojis or images for kid-friendly systems
- Label by use, not just category (e.g., "Everyday Snacks" vs. "Food")
- Try erasable chalk labels if your contents rotate seasonally

Zones to label:

- Pantry shelves
- Cleaning bins
- Kids' toys
- Art supplies
- Office files
- First aid

Labels help others in your home use your system without you explaining it—every single time.

Weekly Maintenance Map

Here's how to keep your systems flowing without starting over each month.

Day	Focus System	Maintenance Task
Monday	Kitchen	Toss expired items, wipe fridge shelf
Tuesday	Bathroom	Refill supplies, check towels
Wednesday	Entryway	Sort mail put away shoes
Thursday	Laundry	Check supplies, catch up load
Friday	Closet	Return strays, toss/donate one item
Saturday	Living Room	Reset surfaces, dust bins/baskets
Sunday	Paper & Digital	Sort inbox, shred old files

Spend just 10–15 minutes per day. This rotation builds flow into your week, keeping systems alive and functional.

Mini Habit Challenge: Maintain Without Overthinking

Pick one of these low-effort systems to implement this week:

- "A place for everything" mantra: Walk around and give 5 items a real home.
- Start a weekly reset basket: Drop in anything that's out of place throughout the week—empty it on Sunday.
- Introduce a family command center: Post a calendar, folder system, and inbox tray near the kitchen or main entrance.
- Simplify your wardrobe by grouping like-items and creating 3 quick "go-to" outfits.

Carry This With You:

A good system is invisible. It works quietly in the background, freeing your mind and time for things that matter. Let simplicity be your guide. If it's hard to follow or remember—it's too complicated. Rework it. Streamline it. Design your home to support your life, not the other way around.

YOUR WEEKLY RESET RITUAL

It's Sunday night. You're not totally sure what's in the refrigerator, your phone is cluttered with unread alerts, and the laundry is still partially folded on the sofa. The upcoming week feels like an untrained marathon. A basic grounding routine can be really beneficial during these times when things begin to fall between the cracks. The weekly reset is about to begin.

Weekly reset rituals focus more on preparation than cleanup. It's a practice that helps you declutter and focus. Before the week sprints ahead, it's time to hit the pause button. Like your computer or phone, your home—and you—need to be restarted to function properly.

A weekly reset zooms out in contrast to daily routines, which concentrate on upkeep. It provides you with an overview of what is drifting and what is working. It involves checking in with your goals, clearing clutter before it becomes a bigger problem, and gently rearranging your surroundings to reflect your ambitions. You can change the way the rest of the week feels with just one hour.

Weekly Tidy Checklist

Start with the basics. A weekly tidy isn't a deep clean. It's a reset—an effort to bring each space back to its functional baseline. Focus on key areas that tend to collect clutter and affect your daily life.

1. Entryway:

- Put away stray shoes, coats, and bags.
- Recycle junk mail or flyers.
- Wipe down the console table or shelf.

2. Kitchen:

- Clear the counters. Put away small appliances not in use.
- Check the fridge. Toss expired items and wipe shelves if needed.
- Run the dishwasher or unload it. Wipe the sink and stovetop.

3. Living Room:

- Fold throws, fluff pillows.
- Return books, remotes, and mugs to their homes.
- Do a quick sweep or vacuum if needed.

4. Bathroom:

- Clear off counters. Put toiletries back in drawers or bins.
- Replace towels with clean ones.
- Refill toilet paper, soap, and other essentials.

5. Bedroom:

- Change the sheets or freshen the bedding.
- Clear nightstands.
- Hang or fold any clothes lying around.
- Empty the trash can.

6. Workspace:

- Organize your desk. File or shred papers.
- Charge devices.
- Review and update your calendar or to-do list.

This cleanup can be finished in an hour or spread out over the course of the weekend. On Fridays, they work in the bedrooms; on Saturdays, they work in the kitchen; and on Sundays, they relax. Some people favor a one-and-done strategy. In any case, adapt it to your rhythm.

To make it more fun, play music, listen to a podcast, or set a timer. Don't strive for excellence. Strive for flow—areas that are lighter and prepared to take on the upcoming week.

Scheduling and Seasonal Resets

A seasonal reset occurs roughly four times a year—spring, summer, fall, and winter—and gives you the opportunity to do things your weekly tidy doesn't cover. In addition to weekly resets, your home benefits from deeper seasonal resets that correspond with natural shifts—weather, energy, routines—and offer opportunities to reevaluate, refresh, and realign your systems.

Spring Reset:

- Clean windows, baseboards, and vents.

- Rotate or donate seasonal clothing.
- Tidy the garden or outdoor space.
- Deep-clean appliances like the oven and fridge.

Summer Reset:

- Declutter toys, outdoor gear, and sports equipment.
- Store or donate school supplies.
- Lighten decor for the season.
- Check air conditioners and fans.

Fall Reset:

- Swap wardrobes—bring out sweaters and coats.
- Organize holiday decor or supplies.
- Clean the garage or storage spaces.
- Check on pantry items for cold-weather meals.

Winter Reset:

- Clear paper clutter—bills, receipts, year-end tasks.
- Donate or discard damaged decorations.
- Review your storage systems before the new year.
- Do a digital reset—clear files and update passwords.

Seasonal resets can be planned in your calendar or planner. Handle them as though they were appointments with your house. Divide them into manageable objectives, such as one project per weekend or an hour every night. Even tiny actions have an impact.

A monthly micro-reset, which gives you just enough time to adjust systems and assess your emotional alignment, might also be beneficial for some people. Consider whether my needs are now being met by my house. Do my routines make me better or worse? By asking these questions, minor issues can be kept from growing into major ones.

Reviewing Your Systems for What's Working

The check-in is a significant component of the weekly reset. Reflect instead of merely cleaning. The purpose of your systems is to assist you. They also require adjustment, just like everything else in life.

Commence with what is effective. Honor it. You'll win if the addition of a shoe basket keeps your foyer clear. Take note of whether cooking has become easier because of your labeled pantry bins. Rewarding achievement makes those behaviors more enduring.

Next, examine what isn't functioning. Are there any fresh heaps forming? Your paper system is overflowing once more. Is it difficult to close the bathroom cabinets because items have moved around?

Find out why. Has your routine changed? Was the flow disrupted by a new item? Did a system become too difficult to understand? Better is frequently simpler.

Adjustment is the focus of this examination, not judgment. Every house changes. In the summer, what worked during the academic year might not work. With a growing family, you might need to reevaluate what made sense when you lived alone.

Make minor adjustments. Consider placing a basket nearer to the area where debris accumulates. Reduce the number of categories you use. Consider labeling it or adding a reminder. Systems ought to adapt to you.

Take advantage of your weekly reset to assess your emotional well-being. Does your home feel peaceful to you? Are you staying away from particular rooms? In your space, do you feel worried or supported?

This is also a great chance to monitor any housekeeping or routine practices. Are you maintaining your nightly resets? Have you gotten into the habit of spending ten minutes in your room every day? If not, consider what's preventing you from doing it and what could help. These minor routines can be strengthened with the use of tools such as weekly planner pages, journals, and habit trackers.

Your home serves as the backdrop for your life and is more than just your possessions. You're headed in the correct direction if your processes make your life feel more seamless. If not, make a small adjustment. Drawer by drawer. One fresh concept at a time.

By lighting a candle, writing down their goals, or just sitting in their tidy environment and appreciating the outcome, some people like to conclude their weekly reset with a peaceful time. This small action completes the circle and incorporates mindfulness. It reaffirms that taking care of your space entails taking care of yourself.

You've learned in this chapter that the weekly reset routine is more than just cleaning. Both your space and your spirit will be reset. It provides the energy you require for the days ahead, keeps your home in harmony with your life, and helps you identify minor issues before they become bigger ones.

You're curating rather than just cleaning with a regular checklist, thoughtful scheduling, seasonal refreshes, and system reviews. You're creating a rhythm that will keep you going. You discover more than just order in that beat. You discover tranquility.

You can take a moment to listen to your needs, your life, and your house by doing a weekly reset. More than just your space, it's time for you to reboot. It's your opportunity to take a deep breath, reset, and enter a new week with confidence, clarity, and serenity rather than fear.

Bonus Materials

This chapter introduces the magic of the *weekly reset*—your anchor when life starts to drift into chaos. These printable materials help you create a simple, repeatable rhythm that brings your home (and your mind) back to the center each week.

Printable Weekly Reset Checklist

Use this as your personal ritual guide—whether you complete it in one sitting or spread it out over a weekend.

Area	Reset Action
Bedroom	Change sheets, clear nightstand, put away laundry
Kitchen	Empty the fridge, wipe counters, and plan simple meals.
Bathroom	Wipe surfaces, restock toiletries, swap towels
Living Room	Fluff cushions, dust surfaces, return stray items
Entryway	Sort mail put away shoes/bags, and sweep the mat.
Trash & Recycling	Empty bins in all rooms
Digital	Clear 10 emails, back up files/photos, charge devices
Mindset	Light a candle, review your Clean Life Vision Statement

Pro tip: set a timer for each room or zone—15–20 minutes max. Keep it gentle, focused, and doable.

Seasonal Reset Prompts (Quarterly Printable)

Every 3 months, go a bit deeper to refresh your space. Use these prompts as a guide:

Spring:

- What items feel heavy or outdated?
- What do I want to bring in—light, color, air?
- What expired things (products, beliefs, habits) can I release?

Summer:

- What systems feel too rigid? Where can I loosen up?
- What spaces support fun, creativity, and play?
- What's adding visual or emotional heat?

Autumn:

- What's no longer working? What routines feel draining?
- What do I want to prepare for or protect?
- How can I simplify before the holiday season?

Winter:

- What helps me rest more deeply?
- What corners or spaces feel neglected?
- What can I clean or clear to invite peace?

Write down your answers. Let the seasons lead your resets, not pressure.

Reset Ritual Tracker (4 Weeks Printable)

Keep track of how consistently you're building this practice. Use checkmarks or stickers to mark completion—celebrate the effort, not perfection.

Week	Completed Weekly Reset?	Which Zone Felt Best?	One Word to Describe Your Space
1	☐		
2	☐		
3	☐		
4	☐		

Patterns will emerge. Notice what brings energy. Notice where resistance shows up.

Bonus Ritual Ideas (Optional Add-ons)

Want to elevate your weekly reset into something *restorative*? Try adding one of these mini rituals:

- Brew a favorite tea before you begin
- Use a calming playlist that becomes your "reset soundtrack."
- Diffuse a seasonal essential oil
- Involve family or roommates—make it collaborative, not solitary
- Set a weekly affirmation: *"I care for my space, and my space cares for me."*

Key Takeaway

Your weekly reset isn't about being caught up. It's about *coming back*—to your space, your systems, your vision, and your peace. Make it yours. Make it sacred. Let it be the pause that refreshes and the rhythm that grounds.

Section 4

LIFESTYLE INTEGRATION

Chapter 10

MINDFUL CONSUMPTION

Two days had passed since the package was placed on the front step. Nobody could recall who had ordered it, what was inside, or why it was necessary at all. Upon opening it, it saw something that had previously been duplicated—a brief impulse enclosed in a cardboard box. It is simple to understand how clutter begins, quietly and invisibly, when you multiply that scene by a few dozen occurrences annually.

Just because we're sloppy or unorganized doesn't mean that we accumulate. Because we consume mindlessly, we accumulate. Consumption encompasses more than just purchasing; it also includes how we obtain, store, and use everything from devices and clothing to emails and online subscriptions. Additionally, our spaces—and our lives—become overburdened when we lack mindful awareness.

Deprivation is not the goal of mindful consumption. It's not about depriving yourself of your favorite activities. It's about paying attention to the reasons behind your decisions, taking a moment before introducing something new into your life, and choosing what will remain consciously. You start living with clarity when you start consuming with clarity. Let's examine how you can change every aspect of your life from accumulation to alignment.

Preventing Future Clutter

Preventing clutter before it arises is the best approach to handle it. Keeping things organized and decluttered after you've done the hard work is the next hurdle. And the first step in doing that is to keep fresh clutter out of your area.

Make an entrance barrier first. Always hesitate when something new tries to enter your home, be it a freebie, a hand-me-down, or a buy. Pose three questions to yourself: Do I really need this? Can I make room for it? Is it superior to my current situation?

This introspective moment produces a potent pause. It increases your awareness of unintentional behaviors like accepting something just because it's free or seizing a "deal" because it's inexpensive. A free thing does not necessarily mean it is cost-free. Space, time, and energy are all used by every object.

Using a one-in, one-out rule is another strategy to avoid clutter. Make a commitment to parting with an old item when you bring in a new one. Purchase a fresh sweater? Give away one that you haven't worn in several months. Have you upgraded your phone? Recycle the previous one. This straightforward exchange preserves equilibrium and controls buildup.

Establish "clutter checkpoints" all year long. These are brief, planned inspections of the most cluttered areas. The trunk of your car, the linen closet, or the junk drawer. By allocating time every few months to inspect these areas, you can identify the emergence of clutter before it becomes too much to handle.

Being aware of your weaknesses is another aspect of mindful consumption. Perhaps it's late-night internet shopping, clearance racks, or sales. Perhaps it's accepting freebies at conferences or gathering leaflets and brochures. Power comes from awareness. Naming your triggers makes it easier for you to take a break and make an alternative decision.

Take note of trends. When you're under stress, do you usually buy? Do specific emails or influencers cause you to make impulsive purchases? If necessary, keep a brief journal. Note what you purchased, when you made it, and why. This makes the emotional aspect of consumption more visible.

Additionally, keep in mind that preventing clutter also entails establishing limits with well-meaning people. Not everything that is provided has to be accepted. You are welcome to turn down freebies or gifts. Instead, you can reroute someone's generosity to charities, gift cards, or experiences.

How to Buy Less and Buy Better

The goal of mindful buying is not to stop shopping altogether. It's about making the transition from impulsive to deliberate investing. It's about questioning, "Does this add real value to my life?" rather than just, "Can I afford this?"

Rethink how you feel about shopping. Start considering it a tool rather than a pastime or a way to decompress. Shopping is not the act itself; it is a means to an aim. If you frequently browse because you're bored, lonely, or celebrating, replace the activity with other rituals. Take a stroll. Make something. Give a friend a call. Take part in an artistic endeavor.

Before you buy anything, follow the "24-hour rule." Wait a day before making a purchase if you see anything you like. Whether it was a genuine desire or only a passing impulse is frequently revealed during this cooling-off period. The following day, you're more likely to make a deliberate decision if you still desire it.

Another effective technique is to make a "wish list." Instead of buying something right away, jot it down when you find something you desire. Examine the list at the conclusion of the month. It's likely that many of the things no longer seem necessary. You can purchase them with gratitude and purpose if they do.

Prioritize quality over quantity. Investing in things that last, function well, and you truly enjoy is what it means to buy better, not necessarily more expensive ones. An investment in a well-made object that you use frequently is always better than one that is less expensive but breaks, clutters, or gathers dust.

Put the cost-per-use concept into practice. A $100 item costs 50 cents each time it is used 200 times. A $20 item costs $20 each time it is used. This kind of thinking causes you to concentrate on durability and utility.

Recognize marketing strategies. The purpose of sales, temporary promotions, and "must-haves" is to instill a sense of urgency and FOMO. There will always be another transaction, so take a step back and remind yourself of that. No promotion is worth as much as your peace.

Additionally, before making a purchase, find out whether you already have something like this.

Does this address an actual issue?

Will I still want this in a month?

Selecting experiences over material possessions is another aspect of mindful purchasing. Instead of giving or receiving material presents, think about offering or requesting experiences, such as cooking lessons, memberships, or vacations. Memories, not clutter, are created by experiences.

Remember your digital expenditures as well. Apps, services, and subscriptions pile up, both monetarily and emotionally. Check your accounts for recurring charges once a month. Do you think I'm using this? Do I still think it's valuable? What no longer serves you should be canceled.

Digital Clutter: Inboxes, Apps, Files

Physical clutter is only part of the equation. Digital clutter is as draining—and frequently more insidious. Because it doesn't take up physical space, we tolerate it longer. But a jumbled email, incessant notifications, or untidy files can create a mental cacophony that's equally as irritating as a filthy space.

Start with your email. Most inboxes are full of newsletters, updates, promotions, and spam. An easy method is to declare "email bankruptcy." Archive or remove everything older than a month and start again. Then, set up a weekly inbox clean-out time—15 minutes to delete, respond, or file.

Unsubscribe aggressively. Use a program like Unroll. Me or manually browse through your email and remove yourself from newsletters and mailing lists you never read. Every unsubscribe is a gift to your future attention span.

Create folders or labels to sort essential messages. Use filters to auto-archive or tag emails from specified senders. Aim to keep your inbox as a to-do list, not a storage facility. If something doesn't need action, it doesn't need to stay front and center.

Take care of your digital assets and desktops. Make a system that reflects your life, with folders for tasks, work, personal, and money. Give files unambiguous names. Use dates. Don't just throw everything in the "Documents" folder. Time and frustration are saved by clarity.

Although cloud storage services like Dropbox, iCloud, and Google Drive might be useful, they also require upkeep. Plan to evaluate files during certain seasons. Eliminate unnecessary downloads, old documents, and duplicates. Make regular backups of crucial files.

You should also pay attention to your phone. Examine your apps and remove those that you haven't used in the last three months. Rearrange your home screen so that it only has the tools you use the most. Disable pointless alerts; they divert your attention and add to the digital cacophony.

Digital images may also be too much to handle. Our galleries are overflowing with thousands of photos, memes, screenshots, and duplicates. Begin by removing photos that are obviously poor, such as fuzzy images, unintentional photos, or duplicates. Make albums based on topics or occurrences. Make a backup copy of your favorites and print some. Allow your memories to reside somewhere besides your phone.

Selecting content that captures your interest is the foundation of mindful digital usage. Establish limits on screen time. Employ focus modes. Regularly disconnect. Just as much as your space requires breathing room, so does your head.

Living Lighter, Consuming Smarter

Consuming mindfully is a habit, not an ideal. It involves growing more conscious of the connection between your life's experiences and how they impact your energy, time, and tranquility. It's making the decision to be intentional while society encourages you to be reactive.

Try incorporating a few thought-provoking questions into your week from now on, such as: What did I buy this week, and why?

Which subscription or digital tool did I use, and was it worthwhile?

Do I already regret bringing anything into my house?

These inquiries are not shameful. Curiosity only. They mold your habits over time. They make the interval between impulse and action stronger. They assist you in creating a life that is not just cleaner but also feels more coherent.

Being mindful doesn't need you to live a minimalist lifestyle. All you need to do is look within. Listen carefully before selecting "buy." Before you click "add to cart," think. Take a moment before answering "yes" to anything else.

This is how clutter-free living may be sustained—not by strict regulations but by deliberate decisions. It's about keeping your place intact, safeguarding your energy, and ensuring that your surroundings reflect your ideals.

You are invited to be the gatekeeper of your life through mindful consumption. You have power over what comes into, remains in, and affects you. You improve as a steward of your time, your space, and your tranquility with every tiny, deliberate decision you make.

As you develop mindful eating habits, you'll notice a comparable change in your surroundings. It will feel lighter in your house. You'll feel more deliberate in your routines. Instead of feeling disorganized, your relationship with your possessions will feel grounded in clarity.

You don't need to finish everything at once. You don't need to make it flawless. But every second you take to think things through, every question you ask, every item you decide not to purchase—that's progress. That has a lot of power. That is an example of conscientious consumption.

Chapter 11

FAMILY & ROOMMATE BUY-IN

You didn't own the socks on the floor of the living room. The stack of unopened mail on the kitchen counter and the cereal bowls on the coffee table weren't either. All of that, though, somehow made the space seem like your issue. You're not alone if you've ever wandered around your house wondering how to maintain organization when everything seems to be against you. Being the only one in control makes clean living easy, but most of us share a home with roommates, spouses, or children. And that makes all the difference.

It's not about imposing your methods or making your house a rigid place if you want to get people to support your decluttering and organizing efforts. It's about establishing transparency, enticing collaboration, and honoring everyone's demands, including your own. Perfection is not necessary to have a calm, well-organized home. Collaboration is necessary.

This chapter serves as your manual for gaining support. You'll discover how to create systems that genuinely benefit everyone, how to express your demands without being pestered, and how to promote shared responsibility in your living area. Individual habits develop into harmonious routines here, regardless of whether you live with family or friends.

Getting Others on Board Without Nagging

Asking for assistance and taking charge of the house is a thin line. Resentment grows when one person bears an excessive amount of the responsibility for organizing, cleaning, and keeping the home. However, frequent reminders, nudges, or reprimands seldom result in change. So, how can you engage others without coming across as repetitive?

Instead of starting a fight, start a conversation. Share your feelings on the space's existing condition rather than pointing out what someone hasn't done. The statement "When the counter is cluttered, I feel overwhelmed starting dinner" works better than "Why can't you ever clean up?" The first one evokes sympathy. Defensiveness is triggered by the second.

Make sure your requests are clear and practical. "Keep the house clean" lacks specificity. The instruction "Put your shoes in the closet when you get home" is very clear. When people are clear about what is expected of them, they respond more effectively.

Pay attention to the timing. Avoid bringing up the topic of shared space during a heated argument or out of frustration. Select a neutral time when everyone is relaxed and forthcoming. "Can we talk about how we manage the living room?" you might ask. I believe we can all live in greater peace.

Use the pronoun "we" to encourage cooperation. "Let's find a way to make mornings less chaotic" is a tactful request to work out a common issue. It is open to all. It's cooperative. Additionally, it lessens the likelihood of blame.

Ask questions if you encounter opposition. "What would make it easier for you to keep your side of the closet organized?" Alternatively, "Is there a reason this system isn't working for you?" The tone changes from authoritative to inquisitive as a result.

Positive reinforcement has a significant impact. When someone else contributes, acknowledge them. Even though it only takes a second to say, "Thanks for wiping the counters—it makes the whole kitchen feel better," it starts a positive feedback loop.

Lastly, set an example for the behavior you wish to observe. Speech is not as powerful as consistency. Others are more inclined to follow your lead if you are dedicated to your own systems. People frequently desire to participate when they see results.

Make it as easy as possible to participate. The likelihood that someone will complete a task increases with ease. Asking a child to sort through a dozen cleaning bins is not appropriate. You shouldn't expect a partner to adhere to a complex labeling scheme that they weren't involved in creating. Don't complicate things. A system will be more successful if it is easier to use.

Kid-Friendly and Partner-Friendly Strategies

Each household member has unique requirements, motives, and capacities. What one individual finds frustrating may irritate another. Cooperation is more likely to be sustained when you personalize your approach, particularly when working with children and partners.

Let's begin with children. Making them into minimalist superheroes is not the aim. Its purpose is to foster self-assurance, accountability, and regard for communal areas.

For toddlers and young children:

- Use visual cues. Bins with pictures of toys help them learn where things go.
- Make clean-up a game. Set a timer and play music. Challenge them to beat the clock.
- Offer choices. "Do you want to put away the blocks or the books?" gives them a sense of control.
- Celebrate effort. A simple "You did a great job helping!" reinforces participation.
- Keep storage accessible. Low shelves, open-top baskets, and labeled bins empower kids to tidy without needing assistance.

For school-age kids:

- Create a routine. A five-minute tidy-up before dinner becomes a normal part of the day.
- Involve them in decisions. Let them help organize their toys or set up their homework space.
- Give them responsibility zones. One child manages the pet feeding station, and another the bathroom countertop. Ownership fosters pride.
- Use rewards strategically. Not every task needs a prize, but a sticker chart or points toward a fun outing can motivate consistent effort.

For teens:

- Respect their space. Instead of insisting on your standards, agree on what's non-negotiable. Maybe the rest of the room can be messy if common areas are kept clean.
- Talk about impact. Link organization to their goals—more time for friends, less stress in the morning.
- Avoid micromanaging. Let them try their own systems, even if they're imperfect.
- Frame conversations around independence. "Keeping your space organized helps you feel more in control—especially when life gets hectic."

With partners, the dynamic is different but equally nuanced. The key is collaboration, not control.

- Identify strengths. Maybe one of you is better at planning, and the other is better at execution. Use those strengths rather than trying to split everything 50/50.
- Set shared goals. Talk about why a calm home matters. Is it to reduce stress? Create more time together? Aligning on the "why" builds motivation.
- Divide by zones or tasks. One person handles the laundry, and the other handles the kitchen. Or one does mornings, the other evenings. Clear roles prevent miscommunication.

- Avoid scorekeeping. Keeping a tally leads to resentment. Instead, revisit responsibilities together every few weeks and adjust as needed.

You may need to renegotiate at times. Schedules, health, and jobs all change in life. Communication and adaptability are crucial. Saying, "This system used to work, but it doesn't now," is acceptable. Can we go over it again?

Make organization a shared experience rather than a chore to foster respect for one another's time and work. As a family or couple, try setting a timer for 20-minute resets or doing some weekend decluttering. In a supportive setting, shared duties can transform from chores into time spent connecting.

Honor accomplishments, no matter how minor. Have you finished arranging the pantry? Enjoy a movie night as a reward. Did children tidy their room on their own initiative? Accolades have a big impact. Small triumphs create momentum and habits.

Shared Space Agreements

Agreements for shared space are not contracts. They are dialogues. These are unofficial understandings that improve clarity, lessen disputes, and give structure. Consider these to be your home's operating guidebook.

Start by determining the common areas, such as living rooms, kitchens, bathrooms, and entrances. Find out what's working, everyone. What isn't? Where is the source of our stress? Where do we need more precise rules?

Then, co-create some basic expectations. Examples might include:

- Dishes are rinsed and put in the dishwasher, not left in the sink.
- Shoes stay by the front door or in closets.
- Mail is sorted weekly, not piled on the table.
- Bathrooms are wiped down after use.
- Common areas are tidied each evening.

Agreements should be brief and constructive. Stating, "Don't leave your stuff everywhere," advise, "Return items to their home after use."

Put the agreement in a visible place, such as a dry-erase board, a shared app, or the refrigerator. To recall and concentrate, not to condemn or disgrace.

Check in frequently. Are the agreements effective? Are they equitable? Do you need to make any changes? Having a brief "household huddle" once a month keeps everyone engaged.

For roommates, agreements might include:

- Shared cleaning responsibilities by week or task.
- Quiet hours or guest policies.
- Respecting personal storage boundaries.
- Creating a budget for shared supplies like paper towels or dish soap.

Clear expectations should be written down early on for the benefit of roommates. Try using a shared spreadsheet or whiteboard for task rotation. Shared space agreements work best when they are realistic and flexible; if they feel like a list of chores, they will be ignored; if they feel like a tool for harmony, they will be embraced. If someone consistently disregards the agreements, get back to communication. Ask what's making it difficult. Offer support. Avoid shame. Most people want to contribute; sometimes, they just forget. Sometimes, a system that worked no longer fits the stage of life you're in. Reset expectations without placing blame. A few words can change the entire dynamic: "What do you think would make this feel easier next week?"

Creating a Culture of Support

Getting buy-in is a continuous process. It's a culture. People who live with you are more likely to contribute when they feel valued, heard, and seen. Everyone is valuable when they play a part.

Integrate organization with the character of your home. Not flawless. Not simplicity. But consideration. Establish routines for resets. Honor significant decluttering accomplishments. Honor all contributions, no matter how tiny.

Encourage comments. Find out why a system isn't functioning. Listen to someone who is frustrated. When everyone's opinion counts, a supportive culture develops.

Learn by doing. Teach children how to fold clothes. Demonstrate the label system to your roommates. Instead of giving partners a list, invite them to participate in the process.

Be gracious. Everybody has days off. Everyone forgets. Community is more important than conformity. Mutual regard serves as the cornerstone, and everything else falls into place.

Develop empathy. Clutter may not be immediately apparent to someone who grew up in a chaotic household. Organizing tasks might be overwhelming for someone who suffers from anxiety. Cooperation improves, and your relationship is strengthened when you are curious rather than critical.

To stay motivated, use visual progress. Pictures of the before and after. On the refrigerator is a checklist. A common accomplishment jar is used in which each person records one activity they completed during the week. Pride is bolstered by progress.

Keep in mind that shared living is a dynamic that changes with time. What is effective now may not be in the future. It's alright. Make your systems more adaptable. Roles should be adjusted. Review the agreements. Continue to communicate.

Fundamentally, family and roommates The goal of buy-in is not to force others to follow your lead. It's about fostering an atmosphere in which everyone is encouraged to make contributions to the common good. The benefits extend beyond simply having cleaner countertops when your house becomes a communal manifestation of love, care, and respect. One thoughtful moment at a time, you're cultivating a collaborative culture rather than merely setting up a space.

Chapter 12

WHEN LIFE GETS MESSY

Silence had fallen in the home, but not in a pleasant way. The quiet that follows a frenzy, the quiet that descends after a week of unopened mail, fast food containers, missing laundry, and unfinished to-do lists. There were heaps of dishes. Dust stuck to things. Everywhere you looked, the weight of the week was evident. This was neither negligence nor indolence. Life was happening here quickly and hard. It's the kind of stretch that makes even the neatest house feel like it's on the verge of disarray.

That's what this chapter is for. The ones that follow exhaustion, stress, holidays, or illness. These are the ones where reality starts to overwhelm the processes you put in place, no matter how well-meaning they were. Because, let's face it, things get messy in life. And when it does, rehabilitation is more important than perfection.

There is no set state for having a tidy home. It has a beat. Additionally, our surroundings fluctuate, just like our mental and physical well-being. Things are in sync sometimes. They aren't always. The good news? You can always start over. This chapter offers your permission to be human—and your guide to getting back on your feet, regardless of whether you need a complete reset or just a 20-minute rescue plan.

How to Reset After Illness, Holidays, Stress, or Burnout

The most crucial thing is how you re-enter your routines once life throws them off. The full-scale organization might be intimidating and unsustainable if you go right in. Rather, see your reset as a soft comeback—a method to bring peace back into your environment without exerting more strain.

Rest first, then take action. Don't start cleaning floors if you're recuperating from an illness, burnout, or emotional overload. Drink some water first. Going for a stroll. Taking a deep breath. Reestablishing contact with your energy before focusing it.

Proceed to reconnection after that. Go around each room of your house and observe without passing judgment to re-establish a connection with it. Take note of what is demanding your attention, what feels heavy, and what feels abandoned. You're only getting conscious; you're not yet repairing anything.

Select one anchor area now. This location has the biggest impact on your emotions. It's the kitchen for many. For some, it's the entrance or the bed. First, just concentrate on that space. Avoid trying to do too much at once. Simply choose the one area that, when reset, will provide the most sense of relief.

Make it clear. Gently. Take out the trash. Put dishes in stacks. Clean the counters. Prepare the bed. Mop the floor. Just restore functionality; don't worry about thorough cleaning. Bring about a tiny moment of visual tranquility.

Create a cascading effect from there. You'll probably feel more comfortable transitioning onto the next anchor area once the first one is comfortable. The restroom counter might be the cause. The laundry pile might be the cause. Allow yourself to be carried by momentum.

Set a timer for 15 minutes in each area if the entire house seems overwhelming. By doing this, you prevent your reset from becoming yet another cause of fatigue. As you proceed, keep a donation box and garbage bag close by. Avoid overanalyzing; if something seems cluttered, it most likely is.

Slowly resume your routines. Choose a one-morning routine and one evening reset to reestablish first rather than attempting to reestablish all of your habits at once. Perhaps it's cleaning the sink and making the bed. Your day is anchored by these minor triumphs.

Be kind to yourself for not doing it. You are not defined by that heap of laundry. A stack of papers doesn't either. Productivity is not the same as value. Being clean is not a quality of a person. Mess is not a reflection of who you are; it's merely a moment in time.

Declutter Emergencies: The 20-Minute Rescue Plan

You don't always have the luxury of a gradual reset. Visitors are coming. A surprise inspection is being conducted by the landlord. A professional Zoom call requires a tidy background. Your area is disorganized, and you only have twenty minutes. Now what?

Now for the rescue strategy. Deep cleaning and a panacea are not the answers. It's about functional clarity and aesthetic tranquility. Perfection is not the aim. It is a matter of perception.

Step 1: Gather two containers: a trash bag and a laundry basket. Misplaced objects go in the laundry basket. For real trash, use the trash bag.

Step 2: Begin in the region with the most traffic. That's typically the kitchen or living room. Put a five-minute timer on. Anything that doesn't belong, such as shoes, toys, mail, or cups, should be gathered in the laundry basket. Put food containers, papers, and wrappers in the garbage bag.

Step 3: Clean the surfaces that are in view. Stoves, tabletops, and counters. A moist towel has a profound impact. Just get everything back into order without scrubbing.

Step 4: Make what's left straight. Pillows made of fluff. Arrange books in stacks. Place chair cushions inside. Take the bedspread off. A room can be visually reset by straightening, which takes only a few seconds.

Step 5: Open a window or light a candle. The energy of a room is drastically changed by scent and airflow. The space will feel fresher even if the baseboards aren't spotless.

Step 6: Shut doors to rooms that do not need to be entered. If necessary, keep the turmoil under control.

Step 7: For the time being, store the laundry basket containing misplaced belongings in a closet or corner. You can appropriately return items once the meeting is over or the visitors have left.

You can also make this plan a daily routine. Every morning or evening, set aside 20 minutes to visually reset your key areas. This approach gradually gains traction and lessens the need for more extensive overhauls.

Make smart use of the rescue plan. Prior to interviews for jobs. Prior to hosting. Prior to resuming a new habit. It serves as a link between disorder and order.

Long-Term Resilience Over Perfection

Perfect habits are not the foundation of sustainable, clean living. It is based on adaptable rhythms. Not allowing the mess to occur is not the goal. The key is to know how to return when they do.

Redefining achievement is the first step toward resilience. If happiness or rest are sacrificed for a neatly packed closet, then tranquility is not the same. If a clean kitchen breeds animosity, it doesn't matter. Put progress ahead of perfection. Prioritize function over form. Comfort over criticism.

Make sure your systems have buffers. Keep papers in a "grace basket" for when you don't have time to sort them. For emergencies, keep an extra set of fresh clothes or towels on hand. Make sure you have simple dinner essentials in your cupboard. When everything else feels difficult, these small protections make life simpler.

Establish rebirth-signaling practices. Light a candle and clean one room every Sunday. Empty your car's trash every Friday. These little, regular acts operate as anchors.

Don't embarrass yourself when you veer off course, which you will. Which season are you in? What was different? What kind of assistance are you in need of? An inadequate motivation is guilt. Curiosity has great power.

Make space for imperfections in your house. That may entail a basket that gathers trash throughout the week. Or a day without any chores completed. Perfection is inflexible. Resilience is a dynamic quality.

Maintain a notebook in which you record your present clutter, emotional state, and energy levels. You'll eventually notice trends, such as when and why things spiral out of control. This aids in the development of systems that represent your life, not just your goals.

Involving other people is another aspect of resilience. Seek assistance. Assign work. Distribute accountability. You don't need to work alone.

Keep your peace. This could entail declining further events. Letting leave an ineffective system. Establishing limits on your time and space.

Use rituals to commemorate advancements. Give yourself a non-physical treat when you clear a place, like some quiet time, a stroll, or your favorite music. Make your motivation natural rather than forced.

Go back to your "why." the main cause behind your space modification. It doesn't matter if the goal was to bring about peace, healing, or insight. Additionally, it will help you get through the more messy seasons.

When the mess returns, be kind. Since it will, a spotless house is not the aim. No matter what stage of life you're in, this place will always be your home.

The Emotional Impact of a Messy Environment

The mess has a profound impact on your emotions in addition to how your room appears. Mental exhaustion can result from visual clutter. Your brain has to work harder to focus, filter stimuli, and make decisions when everything is out of alignment. Because of this, even a minor mess can seem too much to handle during times of stress.

Imagine cooking in a kitchen where every surface is occupied or attempting to sleep in a room where mounds of clothing are blocking the door to your closet. Your entire body stiffens. Your thoughts are racing. Instead of focusing on what you need right now—rest and healing—you consider all the things you should be doing.

Because of this, taking back your space after life throws you a curveball is about more than simply appearances. It's a self-care action. When you clean up a corner, you're reassuring yourself that, despite everything, you still matter.

Micro-Habits for Crisis Mode

Here are some crisis-mode micro-habits that help:

- Toss one expired item from the fridge each time you open it.
- Wipe down the bathroom sink before bed.
- Keep a "floater bin" in each room where random clutter can go temporarily.
- Unsubscribe from one email list per day to reduce inbox clutter.
- Do a 1-minute reset before meals: clear the table, light a candle, breathe.

Micro-habits don't aim to restore perfection. They help you stay connected to your home and grounded in small wins—even when your world feels upside-down.

Resetting Routines as a Family or Household

Here are a few gentle ways to reset with others:

- **Hold a Reset Huddle**: a 10-minute family conversation.
- **Use Music and Timers**: clean with energy and a built-in stop point.
- **Assign Reset Roles**: make tidying fun, not forced.
- **Celebrate Together**: small wins deserve joyful rewards.

Emotional Clutter During Life Transitions

Let go of:

- Clothes from a former version of yourself.
- Journals that anchor you in pain.
- "Someday" items that weigh on your present.

Let your space reflect who you are becoming—not who you were in survival mode.

Visual Anchors for Rebuilding Calm

Even one clean surface can soothe your brain. Try a nightstand, corner table, or window ledge. Let it be your peace zone when the rest of your life feels untamed.

Letting Go of Guilt for the Mess

- Your mess doesn't define you.
- Perfectionism isn't the goal—progress is.
- Show yourself the compassion you'd give a friend.

Returning to Peace, Again and Again

Mess is part of the cycle. It comes. It goes. And you're allowed to begin again—every time.

It's not the perfect step. Just the next one.

That's all you need.

Section 5

STAYING MOTIVATED FOR THE LONG HAUL

Chapter 13

TRACKING YOUR PROGRESS

Once jammed shut with old batteries and expired coupons, the drawer now glides softly open to expose trays that are properly sectioned. Clean lines and a clear purpose greet you at the entrance that once gathered shopping bags and wayward shoes. However, there comes a point—a pause—where the mind asks, "Am I really making progress?" in the middle of the still-progressing voyage.

Even after the garbage bags have been removed, the containers have been labeled, and the pandemonium has begun to subside, the question still creeps in. Because progress doesn't always feel evident when it's experienced on a daily basis. The changes are not noticeable. Sometimes, the results are just visible to you. For this reason, tracking is important.

Monitoring your progress is essential to maintaining momentum, whether you're cleaning out your home, changing ingrained behaviors, or redefining your relationship with possessions. It's how you collect evidence of your work, maintain your focus on your "why," and honor the things that aren't always visible.

This chapter serves as your manual for developing self-buy-in so that you may use practical, relatable strategies to stay motivated, reflect deeply, and appreciate your progress. Because how you feel in the space is more important than the spotless room or the marked basket. Following the journey is the best way to witness that change takes place.

Before/After Photos, Habit Tracking, Mood Journaling

Not all advancements come with a lot of fanfare. It can be quiet at times. A change in the room's scent after cleaning the surfaces. When you look at a freshly cleared area, you experience a moment of silence. Unless you're paying attention, these changes may be so subtle that you hardly notice them.

This is when tracking is useful. It highlights those small victories.

Let's begin with pictures. A high-end camera or a carefully planned background is not necessary. Simply snap a photo of the area you're about to reset, such as your bathroom counter, garbage drawer, or nightstand. Take another after your session. Sharing it is not required of you. These photos represent personal achievements. They serve as a reminder: "I did this."

You will eventually be able to view the voyage through photographs. That disorganized foyer is transformed into a cozy and inviting space. That disorganized closet becomes a place you no longer fear. These images provide concrete, inspiring proof that change is taking place.

The same is true for tracking habits. Establish tiny, regular routines and cross them off as you complete them. A downloadable chart, a bullet journal, or an app with streak awards are some options. Simple tasks like "make the bed," "reset the kitchen," or "five-minute tidy" could be included. Something clicks in your head when you see those days stacked up with checkmarks. A feeling of rhythm develops.

You're establishing a ritual rather than merely cleaning. An activity that affirms life.

Let's now incorporate mood journaling as a third layer. Here's where your emotional condition comes into play. Try writing one statement about how your space made you feel every night. "I was able to breathe tonight because the kitchen was clean." "I felt uneasy because of the mess on the counter." Avoid overanalyzing it. Simply observe how you feel about your surroundings.

Patterns start to show themselves over time. The practices that make you feel lighter will become apparent to you. Which areas are peaceful? Which messes sap your vitality? This emotional intelligence is crucial. It assists you in setting priorities for adjustments that will actually improve your well-being.

Together, these three elements—photos, routines, and emotions—function as a compass. They provide you with information about your current location, past locations, and future goals.

Celebrating Milestones

Without water stops, you couldn't complete a marathon. Therefore, why attempt to change your area without first taking stock of your progress?

In the culture of production, celebration is frequently disregarded. After checking the box, we proceed. However, you start a positive feedback loop when you pause to celebrate a milestone, no matter how tiny. "That felt good," you tell your brain. Let's try it once more.

Setting significant milestones for yourself is the trick. Perhaps it's getting rid of a drawer that has been bothering you for months. Perhaps it's having a clear sink before bed for an entire week. Or perhaps it's finally giving away the clothing box that has been by the door since the previous season.

Put your accomplishments in writing. Keep an eye on them. Share them. Imagine them. Use whatever brings a grin to your face, such as a sticker chart, a note on the refrigerator, or a diary.

Then give them a celebration.

Not with additional items. But with tangible benefits. A stroll through your preferred park. A distraction-free cup of coffee in silence. A bath of bubbles. An episode of a podcast that you have been keeping. Instead of complicating the habit, let the reward strengthen it.

The key to celebrating is emotional momentum. It's the pause before the subsequent action. "You did something hard, and I see you" is a nod to your inner self.

How to Course Correct Without Shame

No matter how diligent or dedicated you are, you will fall off track. It's not a matter of "if"— it's "when. So, how are you going to react?

When systems fail, a lot of people fall into the shame trap. Once more, the mail stacks up. The dishes are piled high. The door to the closet won't shut. According to the voice, "I ruined everything." However, that is trauma speaking, not the truth. Additionally, you have the ability to change the story.

Let's normalize the fact that being off course is a natural part of the process. It's actually a component of long-term success because resilience comes from understanding how to bounce back, not from doing everything perfectly.

Begin by impartially watching. Why did the backslide occur? Was it tension? Weary? Go? Illness? Or was it just life growing unpredictable, as life always does?

After that, make minor adjustments. Avoid attempting to catch up on everything at once. Burnout is the sole result of that. Start small instead. Just one thing. One victory. Just one breath.

Write a "Rescue Routine" for the future version of yourself. Something brief and straightforward. For instance:

Make the coffee table clear.

- Clean the counters in the kitchen.
- Collect the rubbish that is visible.
- Fold a single wash load.

Open a window or light a candle.

Don't hide it. On your refrigerator. in your diary. Within your mobile device. Therefore, you just need to follow the steps and don't need to consider when you lose inspiration.

Permit yourself to make course corrections as often as necessary. It's not a sign of weakness. It's sagacity.

Creative Ways to Track Progress

Although they are incredibly effective, traditional monitoring methods like journals and checklists are not suitable for everyone. Here are some suggestions if you're searching for more interesting, customized ways to monitor your progress:

Jars of Progress: Each time you finish a habit or tidy a room, drop a marble or bead into a jar. You cheer when the jar fills up.

Home Mood Map: Sketch up your house's basic layout. To convey the feeling of each space—cluttered, serene, chaotic, or joyful—use colors or symbols. Watch as your house changes over time by updating it once a month.

Voice Recordings: Not a writer? Make use of the voice recorder on your phone. Share your thoughts. I finally organized the pantry today. I felt as though a burden had been lifted. It's powerful to hear your voice change over time.

Transformation Album: Make a real binder or digital photo album to hold your before and after pictures. When you're feeling down, flip through it.

Milestone Ladder: List the stages you're taking to reach a larger objective, like organizing your entire house. Ascend the ladder after completing each one. Progress becomes tangible thanks to this visual trip.

Selecting a method that energizes you rather than burdens you is crucial. Instead of feeling like just another to-do list, tracking ought to feel like a reflection of caring.

When Advancement Seems Intangible

Even if you're doing everything correctly, sometimes the results still seem elusive. This is particularly true when there is emotional baggage. Even after cleaning the area, it doesn't feel "finished." Why?

Because not all progress is evident, it's within your mental state. Your vitality. You've learned to avoid spiraling when you pass a mess. Your decision to relinquish an item guilt-free.

Keep an eye on such items as well. Keep a journal of your emotional victories, such as "This week, I didn't buy anything unnecessary."

"Before cleaning up, I inhaled deeply five times."

"I refused to bring anything unnecessary home."

"When I could have spiraled, I rested."

Changes in your mentality are also a sign of progress. The realization that "good enough" is preferable to "perfect." The moment you begin cleaning for tranquility and cease for approbation. These are also significant events. Your story should make room for them.

Rituals That Reinforce the Journey

Do you want to incorporate tracking into your daily routine? Make it a routine. Here are some simple methods to accomplish that:

Sunday Snapshot: Take a picture of a single room every Sunday. Write one phrase describing your successes and another describing your plans for the upcoming week.

Midweek Reset of the Mindset: Consider how your surroundings have improved or worsened your mood every Wednesday. For the remainder of the week, shift your attention.

Monthly Milestone Check-In: List one accomplishment and one area you plan to focus on next at the beginning of the month. Examine your jar or tracker.

Rhythm is produced by rituals. Sustainability is produced by rhythm. And transformation is a result of sustainability.

The Real Purpose of Tracking

Fundamentally, tracking has nothing to do with control. Connection is key.

It means that I perceive myself as making an effort. I see myself developing.

Even though the laundry basket is full again, it's evidence that you've changed from three months ago.

It helps you maintain your composure when perfectionism's cacophony tries to overwhelm you.

Your story becomes something you can see, feel, and trust when you track it.

Additionally, it is a radical act of self-honor to track your own genuine growth in a culture that continually demands you to evaluate yourself against unachievable standards.

Take a picture, then. Mark the box. Light the candle. In the jar, drop the bead. Not because you have to convince anyone of anything. But because you are worthy of seeing yourself grow.

Bonus Materials

Sustainable change is less about the size of your effort and more about your ability to notice it. Tracking your progress helps you stay connected to your goals, encourages self-compassion, and highlights how far you've come—especially when it doesn't feel obvious. These tools are built to inspire without pressure.

Printable Habit + Mood Tracker (30-Day Format)

Use this dual-purpose tracker to see how your daily habits affect your mindset and mood. Fill in one small action and one emotional note each day.

Day	Decluttering Habit Completed	How I Felt Afterwards
1		
2		
...		
30		

Examples of habits:

- Made the bed
- Cleared one drawer
- Reset the kitchen counter
- Donated 3 items
- Wrote in my home journal

Use emojis, keywords, or full reflections in the "Mood" column. Awareness creates change.

Before & After Snapshot Guide

You don't need a dramatic transformation to benefit from visual tracking. Progress photos can be deeply motivating—even if the change feels small.

Tips for taking photos:

- Use natural lighting if possible
- Take photos from the same angle each time
- Avoid styling the space—document it as it is
- Snap photos of surfaces, drawers, shelves, corners—not just entire rooms

Pair your "after" photos with a journal entry or a single word (e.g., "peaceful," "lighter," "mine").

You don't need to share these. They're for *you*. A record of growth. A visual affirmation that effort is working, even when you forget.

Printable Milestone Celebration Log

Recognizing your wins builds momentum. This log gives you permission to celebrate the journey.

Date	Milestone Reached	How I Celebrated
1		
2		
...		
30		

Ideas for milestones:

- Decluttered 100 items
- Completed 30-day challenge
- Maintained weekly reset for 1 month
- Created a home system that actually works
- Reclaimed a room that used to overwhelm me

Celebration Ideas:

- Buy fresh flowers
- Take a guilt-free rest day
- Light a candle and reflect

- Share a photo with a friend
- Create a "clean day" playlist

Reflection Prompts: Correcting Without Shame

Sometimes, progress slows—or stalls. That's part of the process. These journal prompts help you gently reset without falling into guilt.

- What habits have started to fade? Why?
- Is this a season of stress, change, or low energy?
- What has still been *working*, even a little?
- What's one small step I can take today—without pressure?
- How do I want my space to feel by the end of this week?

Write. Reflect. Restart. With compassion.

Closing Insight

Tracking is not about perfection—it's about presence. When you document the journey, you remind yourself that your efforts are real. That even the smallest shifts are worthy of pride. Let your progress be visible, emotional, and celebrated. You're not just cleaning your space— you're writing a new story in it.

Chapter 14

INSPIRATION & MAINTENANCE

For the most part, the house was not as disorganized as it formerly was. The systems were largely intact, the surfaces were pristine, and the piles had disappeared. However, the spark? That was the driving force behind the first great clean-out? It had blown up. Instead of feeling proud or motivated, you felt exhausted as you stood there and looked about the room you had once battled so hard to regain. Or bored, even worse.

The in-between is the focus of this chapter. After the storm has gone and the mess has been cleared up, you're unsure of what to do next. When you feel like something is lacking even after you've put in the effort. Perhaps the seasons are changing. Burnout could be the cause. Perhaps it's simply catching up with actual life.

There is no need for an additional checklist. You must have perspective. You must have rhythm. You must re-examine your motivation.

Let's go deeper than simple shelf-styling or regular cleaning advice. During the maintenance phase, this chapter serves as your fulcrum. We'll look at how to find a balance between minimalism and cozy space that feels like you, how to adjust your systems to the seasons of life (and real seasons), and how to rekindle creativity when the routine becomes monotonous.

Minimalism vs Cozy Living: Finding Your Balance

Some people associate minimalism with chilly, deserted spaces that include just a chair and a plant. Others may perceive cozy living as a covert justification for clutter. In actuality, both aesthetics are philosophies rather than just fads. And maintaining inspiration in your space requires striking a balance between them.

Fundamentally, minimalism is about living intentionally. It's not about living in a museum or getting rid of all you own. Clarity is key. Deciding on what will help you live. Eliminating visual distractions to improve your ability to breathe, think, and live.

Comfort is celebrated in cozy living. It has to do with warmth, tenderness, texture, and an emotional bond with the objects. It's an inviting space that beckons, "Stay a while," and envelops you like a cozy blanket.

The problem is that they are not diametrically opposed. They are partners.

Picture a simple living area with just one recliner, but now add a beloved book, a candle, and a chunky knit throw. That's equilibrium. Or imagine a warm, inviting nook that is full of character yet with thoughtful arrangements, closed cabinets, and light streaming from clear surfaces. That also relates to equilibrium.

How is your version, then?

1. Be Aware of Energy

Ask yourself, "Does this space drain or restore me?" while standing in various rooms. It's not always a visual solution. The body senses it. Overstimulation can occur from too much stuff. It can feel sterile to use too little. Discover your sweet spot.

2. Avoid Copying—Create

While social media and Pinterest can be excellent sources of inspiration, it will never seem quite right to try to fit your house into someone else's aesthetic. Determine whatever patterns—colors, textures, and shapes—in those pictures appeal to you, then make the necessary adjustments.

3. Apply Layers Slowly

Having family photos or artwork is not incompatible with minimalism. Cluttered shelves don't equate to coziness. A light you love, a grounding perfume, or a memory that should be on display are all thoughtful additions to a clean base.

4. Have Faith in Your Senses

Inquire about the room's appearance as well as its feel, sound, and scent. A song humming in the background or a candle crackling could be considered cozy. Silence could be the sound of minimalism. Pay attention to everything.

In the end, this is about selecting a mood rather than an appearance. When you enter your space, what do you want it to say? In each room, how do you want your body to feel?

That serves as your design manual. Allow it to develop. Allow it to help you. Allow it to motivate you continually.

Seasonal Organizing Projects to Keep Things Fresh

Just as the earth changes throughout the year, so too should your house. Our schedules, attire, rituals, and energy levels all shift with the seasons. A natural rhythm is produced by arranging your area according to the seasons, which lets it grow and change with you.

All too frequently, we view organizing as a one-time thing. That being said, your house is a live, breathing entity. When you adjust it to the season, you give it—and yourself—new vitality.

This comprehensive guide offers ideas for seasonal organizing initiatives that will revitalize your house and your soul.

Spring: Reawakening and Light

The return of light, the flow of fresh air, and the general desire to let go of the stale are all signs of emerging in the spring. It goes beyond simple "spring cleaning." It's a rebirth ritual.

Spring Projects:

- Open every window. Let stale air escape and energy shift.
- Rotate wardrobes—store heavy coats and bring back light layers.
- Clean the forgotten zones: baseboards, windowsills, and vents.
- Clear the pantry of expired items and reorganize shelves.
- Deep clean the fridge and freezer.
- Replace air filters and clean ceiling fans.

Emotional refresh: Start a "lightening" practice. Each day, let go of one thing. A belief, a piece of paper, a piece of clothing. Create a fresh slate.

Summer: Simplicity and Spontaneity

Summer is about freedom and ease. Think mobility, outdoor living, and keeping things simple so you can enjoy the sunshine.

Summer Projects:

- Organize outdoor spaces: patios, balconies, and yards.
- Create a grab-and-go zone near the door: sunscreen, water bottles, keys.
- Store school supplies and review kids' artwork and report cards.
- Update your car's emergency kit for road trips and heat.
- Simplify kitchenware: focus on grilling tools and snack bins.

Energy tip: Designate one "no-clutter" room. Keep it clear all summer. Let it be your mental beach, even when life gets chaotic.

Autumn: Grounding and Gratitude

Autumn is for nesting. It's a season to draw inward, reset routines, and prepare for the inward energy of winter.

Autumn Projects:

- Switch out linens—bring back throws, heavier blankets, and warm lighting.
- Deep clean rugs, bedding, and upholstery.
- Prepare holiday décor and simplify what you no longer love.
- Check expiration dates in your medicine cabinet.
- Review paper clutter—receipts, bills, end-of-year prep.

Ritual idea: Keep a seasonal journal. At the start of autumn, write what you're letting go of and what you're calling in—physically and emotionally.

Winter: Stillness and Sanctuary

Winter is rest. It's slow. It asks for simplicity, safety, and softness. Your home should support deep peace and comfort.

Winter Projects:

- Minimize surfaces. Too many holiday decorations can become visual noise.
- Declutter the digital—email inboxes, phones, cloud storage.
- Organize winter gear: gloves, boots, snow items.
- Review systems: are your routines still working for darker, colder days?
- Store backup items: batteries, pantry food, and essentials for storms.

Cozy tip: Put together a "comfort station." Add some of your favorite books, a journal, a candle, and a nice throw. Make this your winter haven.

Decluttering is only one aspect of seasonal organizing. The key is to tune in and pay attention to what your mind and body require at the moment. Coordinating your external environment with your internal rhythm.

Reignite Your "Why" When Motivation Wanes

You will lose sight of the point at some point, perhaps several times. When cleaning once more, it seems like a bother, and decluttering seems like a lot of work. The point at which your neatly labeled bins become indistinguishable.

Your "why" is crucial at this point.

Perfection isn't your "why." The purpose is key.

Perhaps it's to make your mornings feel more leisurely rather than hurried. Perhaps it's so your kids can grow up in a happy and safe environment. Perhaps it's to prevent you from crying each time you open your closet. Perhaps the goal is to restore peace.

It resides in your heart, whatever it may be. You also need a mechanism to remember it when you forget it.

Here's how.

1. Make It Visible Again

Write your why. Frame it. Tape it to the inside of a cabinet. Set it as your phone wallpaper. Create a vision board of what peace looks like.

When your space starts to feel like a burden, reconnect with the reason you started.

2. Talk to Your Future Self

Write a letter from the future you. She's calm, grounded, thriving. She says, "Thank you for not giving up. Thank you for showing up for us. It was worth it."

Read it when you're ready to throw in the towel.

3. Change Your Environment

Sometimes, it's not you—it's the energy of the space. Move furniture. Add light. Rotate art. Re-sent the room. Music. Plants. Sound. A tiny shift can reinvigorate a tired room—and a tired heart.

4. Let Go of "Perfect"

Motivation dips when we believe we're behind. Behind on folding. Behind on sorting. Behind on life.

But you are not behind. You are *becoming*. Mess is part of the rhythm. Instead of chasing "done," chase *aligned*.

5. Remember Who You Were Before

Look back. Not with shame—but with pride. The person who lived in chaos. Who cried on the floor. Who couldn't find anything? That person had the courage to start.

You are that person, and you are more than that person. You keep showing up.

Final Reflections: A Home That Breathes With You

A well-kept area isn't one that never becomes disorganized. It's one that repeatedly calls you to return to yourself.

A spark is not inspiration. It burns slowly. You deserve a place that supports you, says a whisper in your bones.

Allow your house to change as you do.

Instead of being a duty, let upkeep be a loving gesture.

Allow inspiration to serve as a constant reminder of your "why."

You've completed the task. You continue to do it. And you are home, no matter how lengthy the trip.

Bonus Materials

The beauty of this chapter is that it focuses on *keeping the spark alive*. Clean living is not a one-time project—it's a rhythm. These printable tools help you embrace that rhythm with joy, intention, and seasonal shifts that breathe new energy into your space and your mindset.

Printable "Home Inspiration Statement"

This is a powerful way to re-anchor yourself when your systems feel stale. It's not just about what you want your home to look like—but how you want to *feel* in it, season after season.

Fill in the blanks:

My home is a place where I feel _____ (calm, energized, loved, inspired).

I want it to reflect _____ (my values, my lifestyle, my future).

I feel most peaceful when _____ (surfaces are clear, light is warm, routines are simple).

I will revisit this vision every _____ (month, season, Sunday, etc.) to reconnect with what matters most.

Post it in your journal, command center, or planner as a gentle reminder when motivation dips.

Seasonal Refresh Worksheet (4x per year)

Use this printable worksheet every three months to breathe new life into your space.

Season	What Feels Stale?	What Do I Want to Feel?	1 Space to Refresh	1 Ritual to Recommit To
Spring				
Summer				
Autumn				
Winter				

Keep this worksheet in your binder or home journal. Use it as a compass when things feel off.

Mini Tracker: Motivation Touchpoints

These are non-visual reminders of why you started. Use this tracker to reconnect with your "why" once per week.

Week	One Thing That Reminded Me Why I Started	Emotion Felt	The Action I Took After
1			
2			
3			
4			

Your reminder could be a quiet morning, a peaceful corner, a kind compliment from a guest, or the simple act of finding your keys without stress. Let those small moments refuel you.

Mini Challenge: Cozy + Clear

Over 5 days, blend minimalism with coziness in a way that honors your style and your needs.

Day	Focus	Task
1	Light	Add one soft light source (lamp, candle, fairy lights)
2	Texture	Add a cozy touch to one area—throw, cushion, rug
3	Space	Clear one surface completely for breathing room
4	Meaning	Highlight one meaningful object (photo, book, gift)

| 5 | Reset | Play calming music and reset your favorite zone slowly |

This challenge helps balance visual calm with emotional warmth—a key to sustainable inspiration.

Vision Reconnect Journal Prompts

Use these when your motivation dips or when you feel disconnected from your home:

- What part of my space feels most like *me* right now?
- What's one area that feels disconnected from who I'm becoming?
- If my home could say one thing to me today, what would it be?
- What do I need *more* of in my space? What do I need *less* of?
- What does inspiration look like in this season of life?

There are no wrong answers—only deeper understanding.

Final Thought

Inspiration doesn't have to be loud or dramatic. Sometimes, it's in the light, hitting a clean corner. The quiet sigh of a freshly reset couch. The warmth of a space that knows you—and grows with you. Let maintenance become a sacred act of care. Let your vision evolve. Let your home breathe with the life you're creating inside it.

Conclusion

A CLEAN HOME IS A CLEAR MIND

It could have seemed like any other day when you began this book. There are dishes in the sink. A junk drawer that silently threatens to fill up. Clothing that wasn't quite returned to its rightful location. It might have been a Tuesday. Maybe it was a Saturday morning, and you were drinking coffee and hoping that maybe today you would feel a bit more in control. Perfection is not what you came for in this book. Peace is what you came for. And that's precisely what you've been creating throughout these chapters—not just by clearing out your clutter but also by changing the way you relate to your life, your routines, your energy, and your space.

Following minimalist trends or trying to mimic magazine covers are not the goals of cleaner living. Learning to live with less mental noise is the goal. There is less visual disorder. The less emotional significance is attached to the items that fill your closets and nooks. It all comes down to designing a peaceful, practical, and hospitable house that feels like you. A house that captures your essence and provides room for your future self.

Cleaner Living as an Ongoing Practice

This labor has no end in sight. You will never have a completely organized home. Your life and your space don't unfold in neat packages. Even with the best of intentions, there will always be days when the laundry piles up, the pantry appears to be in a before photo, and clutter infiltrates. Failure is not what this is. It's life.

Living a cleaner lifestyle is a habit rather than a one-time endeavor. It's a method of regaining your sense of self via the practices of clarity and caring. After a hard day, the couch cushions need to be reset. It's allowing light to touch a recently cleaned surface by opening a window. It involves setting a ten-minute timer and carefully navigating the chaos—not to overcome it, but to reestablish a peaceful connection.

You now understand the several kinds of clutter—digital, emotional, and physical—and how they impact not only your house but also your mood, concentration, and sense of self. You've discovered the emotional causes of clutter and begun to unravel the tales, guilt, and fear that have held things in place for years. You've studied how routines are maintained, how habits are formed, and how a single action may change the course of a day.

You weren't expected to be flawless on this path. It urged you to be deliberate.

You have produced more than just cleaner surfaces as you have progressed through each section of this book. You've gained your own trust. The type that asserts, "I have the ability to alter my surroundings." The type that asserts, "I value preserving my time, energy, and personal space."

Now that you've developed a daily routine, you can reset stress-free. You've created procedures that simplify upkeep by classifying what was once disorganized, organizing what seemed haphazard, and enabling your house to "talk back" to you in understandable, encouraging ways. You've established weekly routines that help you stay focused even when life seems to be getting out of control. Additionally, you've accepted seasonal organization as a kind way to celebrate your own growth as well as that of your house.

Reframing Your Home as a Sanctuary

Your house is more than just a set of rooms. It's more than just a place to eat, sleep, or do laundry. Your house is a haven for you. When the world is noisy, it's the spot that captures you. It serves as the setting for your memories and your mornings. And you navigate life more easily when it helps you visually, emotionally, and energetically.

You are encouraged to change your perspective from "clean to impress" to "clean to connect" throughout this book. Should view your home as a place to feel protected, inspired, and completely alive rather than as something that needs to be fixed.

A sanctuary isn't necessarily pristine. It denotes intentionality. It entails asking yourself: Does this environment encourage my desired feelings? Do my possessions represent not only my history or my ambitions but also my current season?

You've learned the distinction between simple and significant, between comfortable and busy. You now know how to combine warmth and clarity to create a room that is not just neat but also vibrant, cozy, and unique.

You've made spaces in your house for relaxation, sustenance, concentration, and connection. You've mastered the art of using grace, not guilt, to express your requirements to those who share your space. Additionally, you've planned for the messy times of the year, such as the holidays, stressful weeks, and days of fatigue, by understanding how to start over with compassion instead of condemnation.

You no longer wait for the "perfect time" to organize, clean, or make adjustments. You now know that it's best to start small, start now, and start over. You've let your space change with you rather than expecting it to remain constant.

That's what sanctuary is all about. Presence, not perfection.

What This Journey Has Covered

Let's take a breath and honor everything you've moved through:

- You started by identifying the emotional, physical, and digital causes of clutter and its effects on your life.
- You learned about the psychology of your habits, including how they develop, why they don't work, and how to keep them going.
- You anchored your house in clarity and purpose by creating a personal vision for your cleaner life.
- You gained useful skills and the emotional freedom to let go after learning five fundamental decluttering ideas.
- To gain confidence, you embarked on a declutter campaign, focusing on major areas and obvious victories.
- You learned to let go with thankfulness rather than shame by confronting guilt and nostalgia head-on.
- Cleaning without fear or drama is one of the little everyday routines you develop that make every place simpler to live in.
- You created areas that maintain their neatness by streamlining systems using labels, containers, and flow.
- You accepted a weekly reset routine—your constant pulse in a hectic existence.
- By reframing what comes in, you engage in conscious consumption and prevent your hard work from being undone.
- You created shared systems rather than individual stress by involving your family or housemates.
- You learned how to reset after difficult seasons, not just good ones, and were ready for the mess.
- You discovered how to monitor your development, acknowledge your successes, and consistently show up.

- You looked at how seasonal refreshes and upkeep may make an organization a dynamic, breathing process.
- Finally, you reframed everything by viewing your house as a haven rather than a burden. A manifestation of your concern. A container for your tranquility.

Your actions are not insignificant. This is change. You've changed how you relate to the things that used to overwhelm you, not because everything is neat anymore.

If You Remember Just One Thing

Take this with you:

Your home should work for you—not the other way around.

Serving your stuff is not why you are here. Even if your closet becomes disorganized again, you are still a success. The dishes piling up or the counters becoming cluttered does not make you less worthy.

It is okay for you to start over. as often as necessary.

The one thing I hope you remember is that living a cleaner lifestyle has nothing to do with the appearance of your house. It's about the sensation. as well as your feelings within it. Regaining your time, energy, and mental space is the goal. It's about developing the self-confidence to let go, to halt, to decide, to come back. The goal is to construct a house that will support you during all seasons.

Final Words of Encouragement

On certain days, everything will go smoothly when the routines become ingrained. When the air seems clean, and the counters shine. Cherish those moments.

On certain days, everything will go backward. When systems malfunction. as inspiration wanes. On those days, show grace.

You have now established a foundation. You've developed routines. You've raised awareness. You've increased your capacity. You'll know how to return even if you take a step back. That is this work's power. It builds resilience rather than expecting perfection.

Do not lose sight. Don't overburden your systems. Remember your "why."

You now understand that every act of order is an act of care, whether it be cleaning a surface or your mind. Peace returns with each reset.

You'll also remember that clean living is more than just tidy shelves and color-coded bins each time you stand in your home and feel your shoulders relax, your breath deepen, and your mind soften.

It is lucidity. It's the goal. It is a haven.

And it's yours now.